No Greater Joy Volume Three

by

Michael & Debi Pearl

Published by
No Greater Joy Ministries, Inc.
1000 Pearl Road
Pleasantville, TN 37147
United States of America

The Cover
The beautiful artwork on the cover is entitled "Open for Business," by Mark Keathley. Limited Edition Prints of this image and other Artworks by Mark Keathley may be obtained from NEWMARK USA, 11700 Commonwealth Drive, Louisville, KY 40299. (800) 866-5566

Table of Contents

The Flavor of Joy 1

Power of the Media Revisited 7

It's the Book's Fault...11

Angry Child?...19

My Little Knucklehead 23

Something Right 28

My Brother is a Brat...30

Rats 33

Potty Training 37

Butterflies and Backdoors 38

The Reconciler...41

What Daddy Doesn't Know Won't Hurt Him...................42

More Potty Training...43

The Parental Root 44

Getting in Tune 51

Rodless Training 53

He's Got Child Training Nailed Down 63

Church or Children? 64

My Two Cents 66

Infant Manifesto...70

Abusive Husband 74

Preventive Training..81

Infant Maniwhatso? 91

The Goo-goo Lady...96

Ramblin..98

My Journey 103

Preface

Our first book on child training, **To Train Up a Child**, has now been distributed in a quantity approaching 350,000. In answer to the many questions we receive in the mail, Deb and I began the publication of a newsletter, **No Greater Joy.** It started out as eight pages but soon grew to twenty-four. It is now distributed to over 45,000 homes.

We found that most of the questions we were asked had already been answered in one of our previous newsletter articles. The demand for back newsletters was so great that it became a burden to maintain an inventory. Thus, we compiled our second book on child training, **No Greater Joy Volume One.**

But the letters continued to come in, and new issues were raised or old ones needed further attention. More newsletter articles were written. So we gave you a further compilation of articles, **No Greater Joy Volume Two.**

It has been over two years now since **Volume Two** was published and the ministry continues to grow. Much has been written in the subsequent newsletters that you may have missed. Therefore, it is with great delight that we give you our latest compilation of articles, **No Greater Joy Volume Three.**

It is a provocative experience to read the many letters we receive daily. One letter will tear at our souls as we read of the pain and injury occurring in a family. The next letter will thrill us with wonder at the miracles God has accomplished in a parent's heart. Debi and I are always discussing, analyzing, praying, and writing. Much has been written that we are not yet ready to make public. In time, as our hearts are settled and our keyboards express our minds, we will address a broader scope of family issues.

We pray that in this volume you will find a little light to direct your steps in the most important job in all of human history—training up a child in the way he should go.

The Flavor of Joy

Parenting, like courtship, must be properly seasoned with joy. Parenting without joy is not only tasteless, it is tiring. Joy is more than the fragrance of the moment; it is the energy required to live life to its fullest. Parenting without joy is like music without rhythm or flowers without color. A joyless parent can no more raise happy kids than a skunk can raise skunklets that smell good.

You say, "But the kids destroy my joy!" I am sure it's mutual. Without aggressive, deliberate child training techniques your kids will be unruly, and your home will be disorderly—sometimes explosive. You will be unhappy, short, rude, and a gripe. If someone were to ask your kids if you are joyful, what would they answer?

In many families the problems are not deep—bad, yes, but not deep. They don't have deep-seated hostilities or resentments, just chaos. Families without enforced boundaries are like intersections without traffic lights. The "me first" attitude rules relationships. When rules are not enforced so as to guarantee the rights of everyone, "road rage" comes home to the family. Like erecting a traffic light, when parents take authority and enforce boundaries, order is established, the tension leaves, and everything runs smoothly. When there is no adequate authority, children are generally too unruly and the home is too disorganized to permit positive interchange between family members. Frustrated parents develop permanent expressions of criticism. The family is marked by lack of joy.

Many parents have applied simple training procedures and gained complete control of their families in just a few days. By restoring order, these parents have eliminated the outward circumstances that provoked everyone to confusion.

It is a blessing to have discipline and peace in the home, but the absence of conflict does not necessarily imply joy. Joy is a positive virtue, not just the absence of conflict.

Some parents are joyless regardless of the circumstances. They may not be angry or unhappy, just joyless. Look at it as a scale, with anger and bitterness on the far left, a stable and sedate personality in the middle, and joyfulness on the far right. Granted, children do far better with deadpan parents who have no joy than they do with angry or bitter parents, but they do best when both parents are known for their joy.

Bitterness is like a plant with a disease. Joyless mediocrity is like a plant without disease, growing in average to poor soil. Joyfulness is a plant rooted in well-balanced soil with the right combination of rain and sunshine. It bears sweet fruit.

The Bible tells us to bring up our children "in the nurture and admonition of the Lord." The body, mind, and will of a child are trained from without, but the soul of a child is nurtured from within, through example and fellowship. There is no nurturing without joy. As the joy of the Lord is the Christian's strength, the joy of the parent is the child's strength.

Children must be joined to their parents by something more than physical lineage. Children choose their role models. They will seek to be like the person to whom they are most attracted. Parents cannot demand respect or admiration. If it is not freely given, it doesn't exist. Joy attracts everyone. Children are not molded by hands of psychology, but by a heart of joy.

Children are rooted in parental attitude more than in proper technique. More is caught than taught. As salt that has lost its savor is good for nothing but to be cast out and trampled under foot, so parenting that has lost its joy results in a family trampled under foot. As parenting without training is chaos, training without joy is tyranny.

Where there is no joy, what is the point? A soldier can endure the mud, blood and pain of war by visualizing past or future joys, but a child without joy is a lost soul. Likewise, one can endure a dull or painful occupation, knowing that there is a sanctuary of joy waiting after hours, but when the sanctuary is joyless, what hope can sustain him? A mature wife may cope with a joyless marriage by consoling herself in the hope of afterlife, but a child can't so resign himself. A husband may deal with a joyless marriage by losing himself in the rewards of occupation or hobby, but a child has no outlet that can compensate for loss of relationships. Relationships are a part of the adult world, but relationships are all the world to a child. An adult without refreshing relationships may still be successful in his career. He can read, engage in hobbies, or just endure loneliness, but a child without relationships is emotionally ill.

Ungratefulness or bitterness destroys joy. If Christ were joy, Antichrist would be bitterness. No matter the skill or technique, as a painting done in bitterness leaves its strokes on the canvas, parenting done in bitterness will leave its scars on the canvas of the soul. Bitterness is like a virus; it multiplies until it infects all healthy tissue. It is rottenness to the bones. If the parent's unhappiness has some other cause outside the child, it will still reflect back on the child. Any unhappiness in the home is going to show up in the children.

Positive creativity is conceived in the womb of joy. God created humans to be happy. Happiness and joy are a healing balm. Joyfulness smiles away all the wrinkles in a child's attitude. Children who rise up a little grumpy and meet a smiling mother are soon smiling with her. On the other hand, children who rise up grumpy and meet a grumpy mother will spiral downward into the pit of misery. Mothers may think to themselves, "I am tired of them being grouchy; I will put the pressure on until they straighten up." Pressure never caused a sapling to grow straight. They grow straight when they are reaching for the sunlight.

A little girl who gets up with a chip on her shoulder should meet a smiling mother who is undaunted in her expressions of delight. If the child is not soon overcome with joy, don't let her alter the mood of the family. She should be the odd one; she should cut herself out of the fun with her attitude. If a grumpy child can change the atmosphere to reflect her bad mood, then, in her estimation, her grouchiness is justified.

Though a parent must be firm in enforcing boundaries, you cannot threaten, insult, or intimidate a bad attitude out of a child. If you become angry, then the child cannot help but view your "discipline" as a personal challenge. The child is offended at your attitude and will respond in anger. The other children catch the gripes and it infects the entire family.

Now, there is a religious escape mechanism you can employ at this point to get yourself off the hook and ignore what I have said. First, put on your most devout and earnest expression, breathe deeply, sigh, let your shoulders droop just a little, now lower your eyebrows and say, "I know I am not happy, but I do have the joy of the Lord in my heart." Now is the time to say that little ditty you learned in a sermon, "Happiness is based on the happenings of life, which we cannot control, but joy is based on our relationship to God." Now that you have separated happiness from joy, you can admit that you are not happy and profess to have an unseen joy tucked away somewhere. Some people think it is carnal to be happy. I doubt that the kids appreciate your mystical joy. What they need is happy, cheerful parents. Your theological joy is all right in a ladies' deeper-life conference, but it is no better than cussing when it comes to raising kids.

Ask yourself this question: Is my lack of joy a result of circumstances alone? If you trained your children to be obedient, would you then be joyful? If your lack of joy is circumstantial, then you should be able to reverse the trend by properly training the kids. Many have testified that after just one day of training, everyone in the family was transformed. When that happens you can know that the symptoms were shallow, just procedural; your technique was off, and so training removed the barriers to joy. Your unhappiness was caused by outer circumstances rather than by inner bitterness.

But if your unhappiness is something you manufacture in your own soul, then applying training techniques will be of some help, but it will not bring the children to where they should be, and it will not give you lasting joy. If your unhappiness is in your soul, then you must go to the soul doctor. Jesus Christ is the only licensed soul doctor. All others are quacks. St. John the apostle said, *"And these things write we unto you, that your joy may be full (1 John 1:4)."* Start counting your blessings rather than recounting the reasons why you should be miserable. Life will sum up differently.

John goes on to discuss the things that bring full joy: *"The blood cleanses us from all sin; he is faithful to forgive us of all sin and to cleanse us from all unrighteousness; truly, our fellowship is with the Father and with his son Jesus Christ; a new commandment I write, that you love one another; I write unto you, little children, because your sins are forgiven you for his name's sake; Beloved, now are we the sons of God, and it doth not yet appear what we shall be: but we know that, when he shall appear, we shall be like him; for we shall see him as he is* (taken from 1 John).*"*

Here is one I like: *"Live joyfully with the wife whom thou lovest all the days of thy life...for that is thy portion in this life (Ecclesiastes 9:9)."* That makes me smile.

How about this commandment? *"Neither be ye sorry; for the joy of the LORD is your strength (Nehemiah 8:10)."*

Would you resolve as David did? *"And my soul shall be joyful in the LORD (Psalm 35:9)."*

Perhaps you need to confess your sinfulness to God and pray with David, *"Restore unto me the joy of thy salvation (Psalm 51:12)."*

God sums up the Christian experience: *"For the kingdom of God is not meat and drink; but righteousness, and peace, and joy in the Holy Ghost (Romans 14:17)."* Religion without joy is godless.

Finally, here is the one we based our newsletter on: *"I have no greater joy than to hear that my children walk in truth (3 John 4)."* This is the greatest earthly joy.

Children thrive on joy. They will do anything for someone who enjoys them. Parents have asked me, "What is the first step to recovering what I have lost with my children?" Many times I have answered, and I have never found a need to revise it: "Look into the face of your child and smile." Let your child look into your face and see someone delighting in their presence. Don't withhold your joy on the condition that your child earn your smile. Who deserves a good friend? Who deserves the Savior's love? Smile your children into obedience, and you will find that the rod is seldom necessary. Become the Pied Piper of joy. You won't have to drive them if you give them something worth following. Don't just smile at your kids; smile into them; smile through them. Let joy flow, and your family will be swept along in the current. ☺

Dear Mr. and Mrs. Pearl,

Let me share a funny story with you. A friend of mine gets this newsletter out of "nowhere," talking about child training. She tells me I would really like it, but I did not think too much about it until she got her tapes. She kept saying, over and over, you should listen to these tapes, they are really good. Finally, she brought me the tapes and I began to listen to them. Within the first 3 minutes I was appalled! I stopped the tape, called her and said, this man is nuts! I agreed with everything you said about training children as well as how to train them. It was your thoughts on public school that upset me. You see, I was currently a first grade teacher in a public school. I said, "He has never set foot in my classroom, he doesn't know squat. Maybe it is like that in the big city, but not in my small town, not in my room!" I went on maternity leave soon after and decided to homeschool my daughter for the year. The Lord has taught me a lot over the past year, including my ignorance! I was always very careful not to teach any of that anti-God stuff. But unknowingly, I did. Under the guise of critical thinking, values clarification, and higher-order learning skills, new age came into my classroom. I must say, you have never been in my classroom, but you couldn't have been more accurate in your statements, even in my small town, even in my classroom.

I know the Lord has a sense of humor, because the same person who thought you were nuts is now just as nuts as you are! I am currently helping 3 families begin their road to homeschooling!

In Christ, B.T.

Power of the Media Revisited

I have new information confirming our former hypothesis as to the advantages of employing recent technological advances in child training and behavior control. For approximately $500.00 you can have perfectly obedient children, at home or in public. If you are budget minded there are ways to get by for under $25.00 or, if you don't mind a little deception played on your children, there are ways to get your equipment free.

Of course, if you read our article, "The Power of the Media," you know that the electronic child-control equipment we are talking about is a video camera. You can get an old twelve-pounder from the hock shop for $25.00, or you can get one free from a friend who dropped his in the lake and shorted out all the wiring. It doesn't matter whether or not you are actually taking pictures as long as the children think you are. We have discovered that a pointed camera is better than a pointed finger. Switching on a camera (or pretending to) is better than switching on the kids.

Just this past week, I purchased a new digital video camera. I took it to the church meeting Sunday to shoot some good footage [for you laymen, that's videographer's language for "taking pictures"]. I was hoping to "do a take" on some kid throwing a fit. In the course of events, I explained to everyone that I would be documenting their child training, and in the process, making some of the parents infamous. After the meeting I hurried outside to try for a Pulitzer Prize winning shot.

I saw several parents seriously talking to their children while pointing to my camera. The children were all soaking it up quite seriously. Well, with fifty kids in sight I was able to capture only one little fit. And it was spoiled when an eight-year-old candidate for an overdose on Ritalin leaped in front of the screaming child, shoved his scrawny face into the lens, and commenced to scream hysterically. He was auditioning, of course. You will remember him as the one that I tied up on the camping trip. The small child, who had been throwing the fit, immediately stopped crying and stared at the older kid. She was out-classed. He spoiled the shot of the kid throwing the fit, but he gave me great footage of a kid that the state of Texas has insisted should be put on Ritalin. His mother has wisely refused, and the kid continues to act like a boy. By the way, I wouldn't have the little knot-head any other way. I wandered around the churchyard, trying to get natural shots, but everyone was on guard. It looked like an IRS waiting room.

That evening, Carolyn, three and one-half years old, was visiting the house. I offered her a piece of cake and she readily accepted. So I lifted her into a chair and served the cake. As I was walking off, she called my name in a tone of supplication. When I turned around, I could see that she had something serious to say. "Mike, I am a good girl now." I had never questioned it, so I was puzzled until the next day when her mother told me of an event on the previous day. That Sunday afternoon, everyone was playing volleyball, and the smaller children were swinging on ropes, racing bicycles, building sand castles, and swimming in the creek. Carolyn's mother noticed that Carolyn was playing unusually well. All afternoon she had not whined, complained, cried, or hesitated to obey. Mother said to Carolyn, "You have been so good this afternoon!" Carolyn responded, "Yeah, I am afraid Mike Pearl is hiding in the bushes, trying to take my picture." It seems I am now the editor of the infamous Cane Creek Video Tabloid. No child is safe to throw a fit or relax into selfishness. Where is the American freedom to have an emotional breakdown? Even a wrong pucker or droop of the shoulders could bring the camera instantly into play.

Now there is a great lesson in this for parents. Think about it. A three-year-old child knows that certain behavior is wrong. The child would be embarrassed to have her behavior documented on video. Parents are naive. Children convince their parents that they are helpless creatures of indulgence. "The child doesn't understand." It is the parents who don't understand. "But the poor thing is upset; she just needs some reassurance." Poke a video camera in her face with a promise to show it to everyone, and see if she is still helpless and confused. Everything comes into focus real fast.

If the three-year-old can control her emotions and responses for six hours for fear that someone is hiding somewhere trying to get video footage of her embarrassing behavior, then she has demonstrated that she has complete control over her entire body, mind, and emotions. If she throws a fit later on, it is because she has an agenda and knows how to get her way. Parents provoke and affirm such behavior by treating it as normal. If you respond to fits of anger with your own fit of anger, you are giving legitimacy to that kind of behavior.

We occasionally have small children visiting in our home who try running their emotional con game on us. It is so completely unacceptable around here that we all just stop and stare in amazement. One of us will comment on the bizarre behavior. Someone else will laugh and comment on how silly it looks. One will turn to another and say in the presence of the kid throwing the fit, "That must work at home; she doesn't know us very well does she?" Another one of my kids may say, "Did you see how she fell down on the floor? You know her tears even look real! Maybe she is going to be an actress when she grows up. Let's all go eat while she practices her parent training skills. Let's just leave her in here. Shut the door so we don't have to listen to her." Once or twice with a response like that, and the kid is humiliated enough not to try it again. Now understand, I am talking about dealing with someone else's kid, not my own. You can't spank your neighbor's kid, especially when it is really your neighbor that needs the spanking.

I will tell you something else that works well. When a child is so emotionally upset that he has completely lost control, lean over and talk in low tones to others in the room, ignoring the child. He will stop crying to hear what you are saying. I am not suggesting that you do this as a regular way of training. It is just a lot of fun, and it will give you a clear perspective on what you are dealing with. Kids don't like to be left out of anything. They will give up a good "spell" to hear what is going on.

Parent, when are you going to grow up and act like an adult? Someone needs to be in authority around your place. Your children know exactly what they are doing, and they know what you are going to do when they start their little displays. If you come to my house, you know what I am going to do. That's right, I am going to take aim at you with my Canon—and it will be loaded. See you on the big screen, as will everyone else! ☺

Dear Pearls,

I wanted to share with you a recent incident I had with my son. Yesterday, we had a major battle of wills. I have been praying for an opportunity to get to the heart of his rebellion, but up until yesterday, I could not seem to find one. He has always been stubborn, but responsive to the rod.

I had put him down for a much-needed nap, but he stood up and started crying (not unusual). I spanked him and put him down. He stood up again as soon as I walked out (not unusual). What was unusual was that rather than 2 or 3 spankings to gain compliance, he continued the above scenario for more than 20 times! (I stood in awe of the stubbornness of this little person!) I cried out to God, and I felt a strong encouragement to go on. So many Proverbs came to mind to back me up: "Chasten thy son while there is hope, let not thy soul spare for his crying," etc. I knew this was the opportunity I had prayed for. The struggle had become to "stop crying," and I knew he could do it because he stopped to listen to me when I would come back in and explain that because he was disobeying, I would have to spank him, etc. I decided not to give him so much time to stop, not to walk out and hope he would "wind down" but to spank on the first whimper, and only one or two spats, since he'd had so many by this time.

I am so glad the Lord strengthened me to continue on, because at last, I saw him "break." And the look of relief in his eyes was unforgettable. He settled down without another peep. Later, when I put him down for the night, he went right down without the usual 2 or 3 attempts to get back up. I was so pleased. It wasn't the issue of lying down quietly I was really concerned about; I wanted <u>obedience</u>. I feel I've tapped the vein of rebellion that had long eluded me. Praise the Lord! This little boy has been so loving and snuggly this morning!

Love in Christ, J

It's the Book's Fault

Dear Michael and Debi,

Our children are now $3\frac{1}{2}$, 22 months, and 3 months. When our first child was 19 months old and I was pregnant with our second, we moved and made new friends with a family that had well balanced, happy, and obedient children. After much pleading with them to tell us their secret, they gave us your book.

To cut a long story short, we now have two relatively well balanced kids. My husband and I are still riding a roller coaster of stress and anxiety with occasional loops of wonderful joy and contentment with our children. That is not what the book said it would be like!! In a way, I feel worse with my pretty-well-balanced kids than I did with the unruly first one. Sure, she threw an occasional tantrum, which raised my blood pressure, but on the whole, I found that I just loved her so much that I put up with those times as being "normal" and thoroughly enjoyed her for just who she was the rest of the time (and even the tantrums I could generally laugh about later).

First, I would like to talk with you about attitudes, mine mainly. I know that a lot of the sulking and whining that goes on with the girls is a reflection of my attitude towards them. As I said before, when I had no expectations or standards for the behavior of toddlers, I was extremely patient with my daughter and her ways, and I just enjoyed being with her. Since reading your book I have set certain standards as norm for my children, and I find that I tend to look at the kids and judge their every word and action by the standards I have mentally set. I don't enjoy being with our kids any more–unless they are having one of their super, well behaved days. I am very saddened and irritated to see how insecure our oldest has become, rather than the secure, at peace child I envisioned at the outset of re-training her the "right" way.

I can see that I need to step outside of our little world here for a while, get a proper focus on things, and renew my perspective. The more disappointed I become with our training non-results, the more introspective I become, which gets me more irritated and disappointed, making the snowball bigger and bigger–I don't want it to explode and shatter us all.

I guess my question to you is how do I get off of this roller coaster before it is too late and I've done damage to the children along the way? I just want to enjoy the kids and nurture them with love and patience and understanding, but I find myself at a point where I cannot deal with the conflicts while maintaining the Christ-like attitude God asks us to have with our children. I am at the point where the hairs on the back of my neck stand up when a child disobeys or displays a bad attitude. I can feel the tension and stress level in my body rise. Though I try to maintain my outward composure, and though I try to speak calmly to the girls when rebuking them and switching them, I think deep down I feel irritated more than anything, because I can't see the training working.

[She describes how the 3-year-old won't take a nap and the other child doesn't follow commands. They spank until they are weary, but it does no good. She says, "We are weary and irritated, and don't know where we're going wrong."]

She continues: The 3 ½-year-old is jealous of the 2-year-old, always wants what the other has, jumps all over us, smothers us with kisses when she sees the younger child coming our way, pushes past the other to get to us first, and sulks when any of the above doesn't work out or when we gently rebuke her for being jealous. What can we do?

The 3½-year-old's attitude will probably mend when mine does, but I find her difficult to hug when she's being jealous or feeling sorry for herself. I think it is beyond a case of discipline when I am feeling like that, and more a time of mending, but how? Why is the switching and rebuke and a general "come," "stop," "go" drilling not working?

The 3½-year-old also claims to be "scared" to be by herself. Even during the day, she wants the lights on in the bathroom and cries hysterically if we all start to go downstairs while she is still in her room upstairs. I am irritated by this, but should this be an area where I just stay with her and reassure her? I have been telling her to just come and catch up with us, but she carries on a bit if we don't stop to wait for her.

We feel very alone and very tired, and we would appreciate a boost of enthusiasm and support, maybe a kick in the backside. These are children God has given us, and we don't want to damage them or our relationship with them, and especially their relationship with Him.

In Answer

I commend you for your openness and willingness to expose yourself and face up to your need.

I often wish I could say tough things more smoothly, but I am concerned that I will not be understood unless I say exactly what I am thinking the way I think it. I fear that if I polish it too much the shine might hide the message. So before I offer some practical advice, I am going to give you that "kick in the backside."

According to your testimony, you were doing better before you tried to implement the principles taught in our book. If I weren't an old soldier, I would feel like apologizing for raising your expectations. Remember, you were discontent with your children before you read my book. You said you engaged in "much pleading" to get your friends to tell you their "secret" to having "well balanced, happy, and obedient children." Obviously you had prior concerns about your child training.

You admitted you had a problem with attitude towards your children, but you seem to have an attitude towards me and the things I said in my book. You said, "Since reading your book I have set certain standards as norm for my children, and I find that I tend to look at the kids and judge their every word and action by the "standards I have mentally set." You talk like someone trying to face up to a legalistic spirit, confessing that your expectations are unrealistic. But know that the standards by which you now judge your children were not imposed on you. If you are uncomfortable with your expectations, change them. Desire only what is best for your children. I give you my permission to throw out all the elevated standards you received from reading our book. You can go back to "loving them just like they are."

But it won't work will it? The new standards are now your own. Regardless of the source, when one's knowledge of good and evil is awakened, it is impossible to go back to innocence. There is a degree of truth in the old cliché, "Ignorance is bliss." You don't become angry when your children violate standards written in a book. Like it or not, they are now your standards. You are judging your children and your own performance by what you really expect in your own heart. You believe that the demands you have placed on your children are possible and desirable, or you would not be frustrated. You are just making one last feeble attempt to lay the blame elsewhere. But I can tell from your letter that you have detected the source of your problem, and you are the target. You must fully face your fault if you are to progress.

If your standards had not been raised by reading our book, you would have experienced frustration all the same. All parents, whether they read our book or not, go through a shift in their expectations, just as you did. We parents demand very little from a one-year-old, but we naturally expect much more from a three-year-old. I didn't teach you to expect more; I taught you how to achieve it. And as a matter of record, it has proven effective for tens of thousands of families.

I remind you of a principle I have stated many times, "If you can't bring your children up to your higher standards, and, as a result, you find that you are critical and losing fellowship with the kids, then lower your standards to the point where you can relax and enjoy their company. It is better to have an undisciplined, selfish, self-centered brat who feels secure and loved than to have an undisciplined, selfish, self-centered brat who feels she is despised by everyone.

It doesn't have to be an either/or. But if you find that as a result of personal limitations you are unable to achieve the norm, then know that fellowship and goodwill are always first on any child training agenda. Criticism, anger, and rejection are Satanic soil, a place to breed rebels and derelicts. You should have given more attention to the section on tying strings of fellowship.

I have been hard on you. But I believe you have asked for it. Despite shades of your attempting to pass the buck, I can see that you know the answer lies with a change in your own heart. You are correct in your estimation, and I assure you that such a transformation is within sight.

Paul the Apostle described his own similar experience of awakening to a higher calling:

"For I was alive without the law once: but when the commandment came, sin revived, and I died. And the commandment,

which was ordained to life, I found to be unto death. For sin, taking occasion by the commandment, deceived me, and by it slew me. Wherefore the law is holy, and the commandment holy, and just, and good. <u>Was then that which is good made death unto me? God forbid</u>. But sin, that it might appear sin, working death in me by that which is good; that sin by the commandment might become exceeding sinful. For we know that the law is spiritual: but I am carnal, sold under sin. For that which I do I allow not: for what I would, that do I not; but what I hate, that do I. If then I do that which I would not, I consent unto the law that it is good (Romans 7: 9-16)."

At one time, probably in his youth, Paul was comfortable in a shallow interpretation of the law. But the day came when he began to understand the implications of God's commandments. At that time, he did just what you did; he accepted the new revelation as good and binding upon his life. But when he tried to obey, the experience was far worse than before he had his expectations raised. He even describes his experience of the law as a revival of sin and death.

The main thrust of the coming of the law was to awaken his conscience to a higher righteousness, a righteousness he should obey, but he found his strength insufficient. In a small way, our book was to you in the area of childtraining, what the law was to Paul. The law was designed to be a schoolmaster to bring him to Christ (Gal 3:24). As a schoolmaster, the law found him wanting and failed him. But what the law could not do, in that it was weak through the flesh, Christ did do through his Spirit (Rom. 8:3).

Dear Mother, you are in that very same place spiritually. You do not need more technique. You need a fresh dose of grace, mercy, and love from God. You need a trip to the cross and the open tomb. You need what I need daily, a trip to the upper room and the filling of the Holy Spirit. Wash yourself in the mercy of God, accept His forgiveness, and you will be different from the inside out. You cannot work this out in your mind. It is the miracle of Christianity to which I direct you.

By way of practical advice, there are several things you need to consider:

♦ **Your relationship to God.**

Without doubt, when a mother is out of fellowship with her children, she is out of communion with God. If there is no peace within, it will manifest itself in your relationship to the kids. We can hide or disguise our relationship to God, but it will show up in the kids. You cannot hide your own spiritual condition with training techniques. There is no way to do the right thing if you are not the right person.

It is not my intention to leave you in a state of condemnation. I am not trying to use guilt to motivate you to be "a better Christian." I am not telling you to exert more effort. There is a doorway to God, not a stairway. We often forget that there is only one way to relate to God, and that is through the blood of His Son. At this very moment, without any preparation of the heart, we can confess our total sinfulness and enter into an experience of mercy and grace. God delights to grant forgiveness to the "poor in spirit."

The biggest obstacle to God's blessing is our own effort at acceptance. We can never find acceptance with God by striving to accept ourselves. Based on the sacrifice of Christ, God accepts what we cannot—in others and ourselves. What we reject, God injects with abundant mercy and forgiveness. The road to forgiveness is not to reverse your course (which is impossible) but to throw yourself upon the mercy of God. Purchase the little book, *All of Grace*, by C. H. Spurgeon. The first chapter will set your soul free.

✦ Your relationship to your husband

You cannot be a better mother than you are a wife. You cannot be in contention with your husband and be relaxed with the kids. It is impossible. You are a whole person, not an actor with different roles. There is a chain of authority, with God at the top, then your husband, then you, and finally the kids. A chain of authority is also a channel for the delivery of blessings. If you do not receive from the chain above, you cannot pass it on to the kids under you.

✦ Your relationship to your parents and friends

If there is bitterness, guilt, or resentment towards your parents or friends, your spirit will not be free to bless your children. If you are giving or receiving condemnation regarding anyone, then you cannot be other than a source of condemnation for your children. Condemnation is like an odor; you cannot direct it. It just oozes in all directions, affecting everyone.

✦ Your attitude toward training

There can be only one motive for training your children—their welfare as they grow to bring glory to God. If you accept pressure from friends, relatives, or society to perform in a certain way, then you are no longer raising up children; you are coaching performers. The expectation of others is a blind motivator. It cares not for soul or spirit. It is for the praise of the moment—not even praise of the child, but praise of parents. Don't let anything, including our book, put you under pressure to display your good parenting. If necessary, be content to be a failure. Care not for your reputation. True training is soul training. Soul training is first training in love, peace, creativity, grace, kindness, understanding, and then self-discipline, obedience, and responsibility. To try to teach heart obedience and self-discipline in an atmosphere of criticism and anger is like trying to make ice in an oven. Shake yourself free from public opinion and personal ambition. Freedom of spirit and joy are caught, not taught.

+ **Your attitude toward life on this planet**

To be a good mother you must have eternity in view. By that I do not mean that you must put on religious pretense, always rebuking the carnally minded around you, and steering all conversations back to the "sacred." A mother with eternity in view will see the value of relaxing with her children. Housework and schoolwork are so temporal, so worldly, unless you can do them in a spirit of fellowship with others. Every day deserves a song and a dance—not the dance of the world, but the dance of carefree feet skipping through the blessings and joy of just being. Dirty floors, clothes that didn't get picked up, spilled milk, and schoolwork that didn't get done will be of no consequence 100,000 years from now. Whether poor or rich, highly educated, or common laborer, the heart is cultivated to enjoy God's presence. All else is vanity and vexation of spirit.

Write down all the things that trouble you during a day, not just the ones that pertain to the children. What is the very first irritation of the morning? It may be very subtle. It may not lead to bad words. You may not even be aware that you have yielded to a bad spirit. Write it all down for one day and then review it at night. Was it worth it? What are your values? Can you realistically expect others to change? Yet, if you change in your values and responses, then all has changed.

+ **Your diet and sleep patterns**

Many, many mothers are suffering from some form of chronic

fatigue. Constipation is killing Americans. Fat is pressing in on the hearts and minds of society. Lack of nutrition and too much sugar are leaving brains running at the speed of garbage trucks. TV and late nights are stealing the family and health. Lack of exercise is wasting away minds as fast as it inflates bodies. Your mind functions through a physical brain. Your spirit lives in a vessel of flesh. The spirit is willing but the flesh is weak. You must learn to bring your body into subjection in order to free your spirit.

◆ **Your attitude toward your children**

We saved this one until last, because if the others are all tended to there will be no problem here. Learn to view your children as people, not kids. They are adults, minus eight to ten years, that you are counseling and encouraging. You have a privilege every counselor would love. You can undo the hurts and hang-ups by removing them before they happen. You are on the other side of the problem—before it is a problem. Your children are your fruit. They are your purpose for existing. You have the highest calling on planet earth. Several innocent souls are committed to your trust. They will be what you make them. Knowing this should give you a proper perspective.

Spend lots of time with your children just having fun. Think of ways to turn every moment of work and responsibility into joy. Win their hearts and earn a smile from each child every five minutes of the day. In so doing, you will not have trouble with your attitude or theirs.

Read the article entitled "Bad Attitude" in our book *No Greater Joy Volume One*. ☺

Dear Pearls,

I am excited to tell you that after only two days of applying the principles in your book, our rebellious, miserable, 8-year-old daughter suddenly transformed into a peaceful, cheerful child. And I feel such enormous release from the bondage of anger! For the first time in our twelve years of parenting (4 children) I can relate to the mother who looks "rested, and her children honor her and bring her joy." Thank you for your godly insights and for the motivation it has brought me to be 100% consistent.

Sincerely, B

Angry Child?

"I do have a question. How do I deal with an angry child? When he doesn't get his way, when I fix a breakfast he's not fond of, he acts angry and blames me. He often tells me that spankings only makes him angrier. What am I missing?"   CH

Michael Answers

There is only one reason why he would express anger when he did not get his way: because on occasion it does work to his advantage. He is manipulating you. The fact that he continues to express anger tells me that he is very pragmatic. By occasionally giving over to his demands, you have successfully reinforced his use of anger.

He knows you feel guilty and inadequate, so he uses it to bring pressure. He knows you are trying to work the anger out of him, so he assures you that your responses only make matters worse. You believe him! So he wins again. Smart kid—dumb parent.

The big problem will come from the fact that he is a little fish in a very little bowl. He is learning to respond to life in a manner that will not work later in life. He controls his weak mother, but the world is not made up of weak mothers. There are some "couldn't care less" people waiting out there, who can also get angry and act quite irrational. Cops are trained to deal with angry boys, even 250 pounders.

I regularly go to a prison that has over 1,400 men in it. Many of them were just like your son when they were his age. No one could control them, that is, until they met a don't-care cellmate and a don't-give-a-blankety-blank guard, surrounded by several razor wire fences. If you don't like the food, and few do, you don't have to eat it. No one will feel guilty when you go hungry. If you get angry and they throw you in solitary, they are not impressed if you say, "That only makes me angrier." Such talk won't even interrupt the discussion the guards are having as they escort you to the cell in your cute little white jacket with your arms tied behind you. One minute out of the cell, they won't remember your angry threats.

Funny thing, 1400 men will go all week without one fight. If you get angry at the wrong person in a prison, you may die with a sharpened toothbrush sticking in your throat. Angry little boys say, "Don't do that, it only makes me more angry." Who cares? When no one is listening and no one is impressed, threats are useless.

I am not callous to your dilemma, but the big problem is in your own mind. You are not free to be forceful and bold. Your son needs to run smack dab into a big, high, unmoving fence of authority. You, Mother, are a pushover, a sucker. You need a renewed mind. Now that I have plowed your fallow ground, I will plant the seeds of understanding.

Let's try to understand this anger. Displeasure when one doesn't get his way is as natural as humanity. If one were not disappointed by unfulfilled drives, he would be without preference, and thus without personhood. Anger is also a natural trait of all living souls—not just fallen men. God is angry when it is appropriate. The Scripture says of Jesus, *"And when he had looked round about on them with anger, being grieved for the hardness of their hearts... (Mark 3:5)."*

Righteous anger is anger directed at injustice, at selfishness. To be righteously angry toward someone is to impute blame to them. It is to hold them in contempt for not acting as they should have. Righteous anger seeks goodness. It is the guardian of love. It is moral choice expressed in one's emotions.

Righteous anger is agreeing with the innate dictates of common law. It is taking your place on the jury to condemn the guilty and then recommend sentencing.

But anger at not getting one's way is something else entirely. Selfish anger is manipulative and unreasonable. It assumes that the ultimate good is self-gratification. It judges all events according to how they personally gratify. To thus be angry when one doesn't get his way is to assume that others exist to fulfill his impulses. To such a one, others are doing righteousness when they comply with his will, but they are doing evil when they don't place his will first. To the selfishly angry, his anger is judgment falling on the sinner for standing in the way of his righteous indulgence. He acts as judge and jury in a courtroom where the only rule of law is the satisfaction of one person—self. All should be subservient to the big I, or all should be damned. A selfishly angry person lives at the center of a small world with all others orbiting for his gratification. He is the manager of affairs according to his whims. The needs of others or the justice of a situation is irrelevant.

Mother, I am trying to make you angry (righteously so)—not

hurt, not guilty, and certainly not timid—angry at the Devil who is running away with your child. You can stop it. You can break the spell. You must feed your son's angry perversion for it to survive. Shake off the senseless guilt and stand firm and consistent in not yielding to your son's demands. When you see that ugly head of self-centeredness pop up in your son, cut it off like you would a venomous viper in your baby's crib. To give over to his demands, even once, is like a mother giving drugs or alcohol to her addicted child. Addictions are not broken a little at a time. They are starved to death. Shake him out of his make-believe, selfish kingdom. Kick him off the throne and never look back.

Now for some practical advice: Cause your son to know that he does not have any say or authority over what foods are set in front of him. You communicate this by never allowing him to veto your decisions once they are made. If you want to offer him a choice before you prepare the meal, that is perfectly suitable, but never allow him to alter events through his anger or ill temper.

You must not be angry. Do not plead for understanding or acceptance in your role as head dietician. Display indifference with dignity. Rise above petty debate and bickering. Like an army sergeant, state your will and accept nothing less. If he doesn't like what is on the table and he is rude, send him away from the table and do not let him eat until the next meal. Do not feed him snacks between meals. Let him get good and hungry. He will then eat baby food spinach and love it.

If you think it is appropriate, and you spank him, make sure that it is not a token spanking. Light swattings done in anger, without courtroom dignity, will make children mad because they sense that they have been bullied by an antagonist. A proper spanking leaves children without breath to complain. If he should tell you that the spanking makes him madder, spank him again. If he is still mad…. He desperately needs an unswayable authority, a cold rock of justice.

I could break his anger in two days. Like a private standing before his sergeant for the first time, he would be too scared to get angry. On the third day he would draw into a quiet shell and obey. On the fourth day I would treat him with respect, and he would respond in kind. On the fifth day the fear would go away and he would relax because he would have judged that as long as he responds correctly there is nothing to fear. On the sixth day he would like himself better and enjoy his new relationship to authority. On the seventh day I would fellowship with him in some activity that he enjoyed. On the eighth day he would love me and would make a commitment to always please me because he valued my approval and fellowship. On the ninth day someone would comment that I had the most cheerful and obedient boy that they had ever seen. On the tenth day we would be the best of buddies and he would obey me because he valued my fellowship and would not want to do anything to lose it.

"The fear of God is the beginning of wisdom." Think about it.

Keep in mind that if you are angry you are wasting your time trying to spank his anger away.

One word of caution: the firm authoritarian demeanor I have described is not the general disposition of a parent. I am describing the ideal parental response to the angry child. When the child does not project a barrier to fellowship, parents should be spending time investing themselves in their children—lots of smiles, mutual appreciation, fun, laughter, creative activity, praise, worship, etc. If we water the tender plants regularly, they won't dry up and need desperate measures. ☺

Dear Mike and Debi,

I have a wonderful friend who gave me To Train Up A Child about a year ago. I had no idea what a treasure I had received.

My eyes were opened the day I finally opened your book. The little Japanese maple in front of the house has served us well the past few weeks! There have actually been a couple of times when my daughter threw a fit or threw food on the floor, and I was about to let her get by with it, but when she looked up at me and inquired, "Switchin'?" I knew it would be a big mistake to be inconsistent with the training! It's at times like those that the words in your book ring true...when an almost two-year-old knows that her behavior is cause for a switching and reminds her mother, who is about to be foolishly lenient.

Thanks for helping put our lives on the right track.

Yours truly, S.G

My Little Knucklehead

By Debi Pearl

A little knucklehead came to visit the other day. I call him knucklehead because he is the type that makes people want to give him a rap on the head with their knuckles. He hadn't been in the house two minutes when he spied my glasses lying on the table. Now I admit I should not have left my glasses lying around, but it turned out to be a great "Garden of Eden" test for the little rascal. He immediately picked up a small rod and started lightly whacking my glasses. I loved it.

His daddy is a fine man who got saved while incarcerated in the prison where Mike ministers. His daddy has become well founded in the Word. Now that he is out of prison, he has had to get to know his son all over again and learn to be a parent.

I could see right off that Mr. Knucklehead needed a cheerful training session (and the daddy as well). First I looked in the daddy's eyes and asked, "May I play Mama for a few minutes?" Since he had no clue as to what to do, he gave me the go-ahead. I miss having little ones, and take every chance I get. I then went to the little rascal, and smiling, leaned across the table and took the whacking stick from him. He gave me a full toothed grin with his only remaining front tooth. He was six years old, you understand.

I couldn't help but adore the little guy; no doubt he depended upon that. But my brains are bigger than my heart, so I whacked him once across the offending hand with his whacking stick, while telling him in a pleasant voice not to bother my glasses. Never losing eye contact, I could tell he seemed to think he had run into a knucklehead bigger and more interesting than himself. I laid the whacker back down beside my glasses and with one last smile walked toward the kitchen. I only got a few steps when he again whacked my glasses. "Haw, haw," I said with a twinkle in my eye, "You are not supposed to touch my glasses." Before he had time to lay the offending tool aside, I had grabbed it up and delivered my next (much less gentle) whack.

Now, if the whack had been delivered in a stressful attitude, he would have been emotionally and physically wounded. If he had been dragged from the room and given time to become hysterical, all training would have been obscured by the trauma. His little brain can only decipher so much information at one time, and the emotional trauma of being taken into a strange room by a stern adult would make anyone's brain short circuit. Instead, he remained at the scene of his offense, getting smacked by the very implement he had used to commit the offense—and this without any anger or emotional rejection. I could clearly see it was a new experience in the little rascal's life.

When I laid the whacker down by the glasses, he first stared at it for a moment, then at me a moment, before jumping up to see what else there was to explore. For the next hour he checked out everything, but when in doubt he would look over to me for the go-ahead. If I smiled, he charged on; if I shook my head, he smiled and backed off. I know his next visit will bring another chance to reaffirm my position as head honcho, but after a few such encounters he will know what I expect of him, and he will have a keen appreciation for my methods. You would think the little fellow would be so glad to be free of the house where the whacking lady rules, but not so. On his way out the door he was begging his dad to bring him back real soon.

Most parents rear their children by some such method as: "Pretend not to see; it doesn't matter; I can take this kind of behavior; remove the thing that tempts the kids; give the children what they desire, etc." But when the parents reach sufficient frustration, they begin loathing the child, and their attitude becomes one of "I can't stand it any longer!" Then the default method clicks in—it's called ANGER. "This kid is a brat; he has done the unthinkable, and I'm going to teach him he can't get away with it!" If you start off ignoring the problem, the only thing that will go away is your patience.

Most parents seeing a six-year-old destroying a pair of glasses will immediately be angry and respond to the child with something like: "What do you think you're doing?" or, "Don't touch those glasses!" Parents then put the glasses in a safe place, and the kid goes on to find some other way of testing adult resolve. When a further transgression manages to elicit a similar response from the big guys, the child looks somewhat crestfallen before going on to the next test of parental attention. By this time, Mrs. Mom or Mr. Dad is sufficiently stressed to begin showing extreme displeasure in the child. In this way, Mom and Dad cut strings of fellowship rather than build camaraderie. So the mistraining process goes around again and again.

Parents convince themselves that the longer they can tolerate the child's misbehavior, the more they express love. Parents fear themselves. They have discovered from past experiences that their tempers are detrimental to the children. Parents waiting until anger provokes them to rebuke the children have seen only ill effects from rebuke and chastisement. They have come to accept the concept that rebuke and chastening are negative events that must be avoided as long as possible. Parents are aware that their frustrated, and sometimes angry, correction does not work good in the temperament of their children. Confrontation brings hostility on the part of the children as well as the parents. Therefore, parents feel that the more they can tolerate it and the longer they can ignore it, the better.

Parents influenced by modern psychology (that is anyone in America exposed to any media or education, including most that is called Christian) take pride in their ability to absorb a vast amount of frustration without letting it boil over into overt hostility. They think they demonstrate their emotional maturity and their love and kindness by sublimating their anger and letting the "little darlings express themselves."

Face the fact: your child's goal is to be self-indulgent without regard to the rule of law or the needs of others. Children are good psychologists. They quickly learn how to manipulate their parents into permissiveness. They learn that if they can make the act of discipline sufficiently unpleasant, and give the appearance of its being even more unpleasant on them, then the parents will back off. Children know two things: one, parents do not want to experience the unpleasantness of conflict; two, parents do not want to make life unpleasant for their children. Knowing this, they see to it that discipline becomes painful for everyone. Furthermore, knowing that your goal in discipline is to make them cheerfully obedient, all they have to do is make your efforts seem a failure, and you will cease your interference and seek a more conciliatory approach—one in which there is compromise—allowing the child equal say in his own expressions.

Parents get so involved in their own feelings, whether of anger or compassion, that they forget the good of the children. Some parents are so shortsighted that they can see no further than the moment. They settle for immediate peace, and the children set the terms for peace. What you must understand is that your children need something very badly that they do not want and will not learn unless you train it into them—self-denial. *"The rod and reproof give wisdom: but a child left to himself bringeth his mother to shame (Prov. 29:15)."* Children allowed free expression turn out worse than a cat allowed free expression in the house.

Going back to our example: Mr. Knucklehead had been allowed self-expression; he had not been taught self-denial. A child proficient at exerting his own will is not ready to yield his autonomy without a fight. He will push you beyond your limit to maintain control over him. It is not you personally, nor is it the thing over which there is a contest (in this case the glasses); it is the issue of independence, the freedom to live without law—capriciously, selfishly. Only when you have allowed a dispensation wherein you have become subservient to the child's will, do you as an adult, a parent, become angry and testy. When you know that you ought to have control, but don't, and you do not know what to do to remedy the situation, the frustration will lead to anger and hostility. Parent, know that from that perspective you will never win. The child will remain in control and never respect your authority until you respect yourself and your position enough to act forcefully and consistently without anger or vacillation.

Children will fight authority, but once you force it upon them, they will be happier than they have ever been. Great peace and security comes to a child who is put under benevolent authority. They very quickly love the adult that forces them into compliance with their own conscience. Like Paul in Romans chapter 7, children will impulsively do what they know they should not do, all the while fighting to maintain their rebellion, yet crying out for deliverance. As the law and the cross, applied in love, subdues the sinner, so the rod and reproof administered in love will give wisdom to the child (Prov. 29:15). ☺

Dear Mike and Debi,

We wanted to share with you an episode of our child training. We have four children, ages 6, 4, 2 and three months. Ever since the birth of our first son, we had claimed the back row of the church (and ran off the teenagers in the process!). This was due to the disruption of our children and the need to take at least one out of the service for discipline. After reviewing your materials, we decided that we needed to have "church training" at home so that our children would learn to sit still in the service. Every afternoon, we sat them on the sofa with a coloring book and crayons. The timer was set for fifteen minutes. If one of them talked, got off the sofa, misbehaved, etc., they were switched across their legs. We did this for one week, and the next Sunday my husband boldly claimed his "pre-fatherhood" pew up at the front of the church. Our children sat there better than some of the adults! We even had several comments after the service about how well behaved they were. We cannot thank you enough for your ministry. We had read all of the well-known child rearing books, but always knew that something was missing. We are looking forward to continuing the training of our children.

Happy Parents

Something Right

Most of our child training examples come from our friends (at least they were friends before we published their stories). Since we are always on the lookout for good examples, we have accumulated a good mental, and sometimes written history of all the families with whom we associate. It has been interesting to see the different family patterns. Some do what they have always done, be it good or bad. Then there are those that have continued to do the wrong thing and have gone downhill. Most of those around us here at Cane Creek, with our advice, have displayed significant improvement in the

training and discipline of their children. The family that once provided our best examples of whining kids has actually made the most remarkable improvements. It is their absolute teachableness that made the difference. Their kids are not perfect, but today their family is a model of good parenting and quality family life.

Just last night, three of their children (9, 6, & 2) were visiting in our home. We had a delightfully rambunctious good time. I even got my beard stroked by the little 2-year-old girl. As we were loading everyone into the van for the trip home, the 2-year-old, trying to move from the middle seat to the back seat, had trouble getting around the end of the bench next to the door. The cold, still night suddenly vibrated with the piercing wail that only a 2-year-old could muster. It was a cry of, "Help me get around this seat!" Immediately but calmly, her nine-year-old brother said, "No, Amy, as long as you are whining and crying I will not help you. If you are going to cry, you will just have to manage by yourself." Amy's 6-year-old sister voiced a similar exhortation, assuring her little sister that she was out of order with her whining demands. Amy, seeing the futility of her display, without any assistance and without further complaint, negotiated herself around into a sitting position. The older brother encouragingly said, "That's a good girl, Amy; see, you can do it yourself; now next time don't cry, and I will help you."

It was quite gratifying to see Amy's brothers and sisters dispensing this lesson in discipline. It gives dual meaning to the term child-training—not just children being trained, but children training children. The beautiful thing about children training children is that the kid-trainer is reinforcing his own commitment to order and discipline as he enforces the rule of law upon his younger siblings. The ramifications are astounding. It is the difference between pounding wheat into flour with a wooden mallet and grinding it in a water powered gristmill. Children training each other when you are not present is like the wonder of perpetual motion.

And talking about sibling harmony, when a 6-year-old is given responsibility to train her 2-year-old sister, she will respond exactly like her parents! I said EXACTLY like her parents. Children learn by emulation. They will mimic your patience, firmness and concern, and repeat the very words in the exact same tone as you have used when disciplining and training them.

One of the marvelous wonders of this is that as children submit to the chain of command and develop an appreciation for authority, they begin to act with dignity and maturity toward those lower in rank. As they come under authority, they assume authority with the same maturity as those over them. The children all become a part of the cure rather than a part of the problem.

When you have a large family with only one overseer—Mother, every additional kid is an increase in the chaos and turmoil. But where there is a chain of command, having thirteen children is as orderly as a buggy full of Amish on their way to church. ☺

My Brother is a Brat

Dear Mike and Debi,

My 18-year-old daughter calls her younger siblings "brats."
My son hardly acknowledges he has a sister. Among the younger
children there is a lot of anger, and they avoid being with each
other. The only child any of the siblings like is the baby, and I
wonder how long that will last. I teach them, pray with them, and
remind them how important it is to love their own family.
Somehow, what started as the children not getting along is now
older children that simply do not like each other. We have a rot-
ten family life. What can I do? What did I do wrong? Help me.

Kay

Answer

Just like adults, kids find it very difficult to like someone for whom
they have no respect. You can't shame them into liking each other,
and you can't preach them into it either. Duty, like the duty to love
your own family, grows mighty thin when you are part of a family
where each one is selfish and spoiled. The only thing you can do is
to make sure you raise likeable kids that kindle respect and honor
from others.

It takes a very mature adult, willing to "die to himself" and be a
martyr, to demonstrate even a neutral attitude toward those that are
repulsively unlikable. Mature adults can harden themselves to the
emotional suffering and sacrifice it takes to go out into this sick
world. For a little while each day they leave the sanctuary of a secure
home to go into the den of the world, expressing love toward the
decidedly unlovely. But they come home tired and ready to relax
around family members whose company they enjoy. But if the family members are more like the selfish dog-eat-dog world, then where
do they go to let down their guard, to talk, find sympathy and relax?

You are fighting a losing battle, seeking to establish one virtue
(the virtue of tolerance) among a tightly pressed group of selfish,

unhappy individuals. You said all the kids liked the baby. Of course they do. The baby has not yet matured to the point of being able to compete with them. When the baby gets old enough to exert his own selfishness, they will turn on him as well.

To live in a social order there must be boundaries observed by all and enforced by all. If your older children do not like their younger sister, there is a good reason. Honestly ask yourself—this may be hard to do—"Do I like the little girl?" Yes, you love her. You are her mother. You tolerate more than do the older children. But do you like that little one that the other kids find so hard to tolerate? What is it that they dislike? There are people that you do not like, and you avoid them. Why? Would you—could you—like them if you were placed in daily contact with them and they continued to manifest the same undesirable traits? Would it help if your pastor told you to like them? What if it was your duty to like them, would that make it easier? What would it take for you to like those individuals? You answer, "A few changes in the way they…." You share the same viewpoint as your children.

I will give you a solution that will work, considering all is well in other areas. Sit your older kids down and ask them what it is about the younger one that they do not like. Do not do this with a critical or defensive spirit, or they will not be honest. Do this with a learner's heart. Ask this simple question, "Children, if you could change five things about your little sister, what would they be?" The things they tell you will be things that need changing. Don't argue with them. Ask them to help you bring about the changes in the little one. Discuss all the ramifications and arrive at a consensus as to how to go about this. The hardest part for you will be something I know you have not done before; you will have to allow the older children full authority to discipline and instruct the younger children. Have them read our book *To Train Up A Child* first. Discuss it with them often. Get progress reports. Stand behind their decisions, unless through discussion (not in the presence of the young child) you come to a modified consensus.

One warning: When the kids tell you what they would like to change in their younger sister, it may reflect upon you. Their reluctance to enter into dialogue on this issue will stem from the fact that to criticize the child is to criticize the way you have handled situations. They resent her like the neighborhood kids resent the son of a policeman who can get away with murder while they are accosted by the law for the least infraction. So, if you are brave enough, and humble enough, and you want a satisfactory conclusion to this matter, then ask the kids to tell you what you need to change in your methods in order to change the child. The kids are more objective than you are. If you can get them to be honest, it will be quite a revelation. If you doubt the answers you receive, and you need further assurances, invite a third party (not someone like yourself, or someone who has always supported you), but someone with great kids and a good homelife. Let that person arbitrate in your discussions with your older children.

You will find that when the older kids are not constrained to be victimized by the selfish little sister, when they can take charge and effect a change, they will suddenly "grow up" in their responses. Your children need to be educated in child training just as you do, so provide the material and atmosphere for them to grow with you and learn as you do. ☺

Mr. and Mrs. Pearl,

I wanted to just write a "quick" note thanking you for your obedience to the Lord in training up godly families. I must tell you, my boys too are changing dramatically from the training. It is so nice not to have to use the rod for every little thing. I can see fear melting away from their eyes. For instance, our 7-year-old son was always "sick" or "injured." So we whipped up some "Cure All" from vinegar, cinnamon, garlic, curry, and hot sauce. The first day he was given a dose of "Cure All" every time he complained about a scratch, not feeling good, headache. He stopped real quick. The next day we took it further. He is quite dramatic, so he progressed from verbal statements to body language. He walked through the kitchen with his shoulders drooping, so I said, "Caleb, you look as if you don't feel good. Have some 'Cure All,' it will help." He took it and shuddered as it went down. That was the end of ANY complaints!!! It's been 4 days or so and he is smiling, happy and enjoying life. What a miracle!! And not one spanking!!!

Thank you so much, Roxanna

Rats

by Debi

I carried my little bag of tools down into the hole where they live and breed. I had been there before, not to this particular hole, but to holes so similar that they all run together in my mind. A quick check told me the child would be born before morning. The business of the moment held my attention until I could see the head crowning. For a moment, time stood still and I was forcefully reminded of eternity. A sob rushed over me before I could get control, another soul emerging to live forever; another living being who would spend eternity honoring our Eternal God or suffering in a burning hell. With this realization, my soul wept in understanding of Jesus' declaration, *"It had been good for that man if he had not been born (Matt. 26:24)."* What chance had this child of living in the light, when all around him the rats that call themselves humanity fight and die? The fog of despair began to dissipate as the baby moved down the birth canal. As my hands reached forth I felt a stir of pure longing, a prayer pouring from my soul, "Oh God, take this child for thine own. Cause this child to know you, to honor you; cause his life to show your mercy and grace." And as I wrapped the baby and put him to the breast of the young girl that was now a mother, God spoke to me, "Your job has only begun: pray, seek to minister, hold them until they know you care, then tell them you care." I took peace in knowing there was hope. But there are so many.

Perhaps it is the seasoning of age that causes me to respond to life's events with either weeping or rejoicing. When someone comes to me in jubilance, proclaiming that a certain family just had their sixth, or seventh, or eighth child, I can only pretend I don't see a sad future. I see their oldest daughter, rebellious, destined for the hole. I wonder if I will be helping her with her first "unplanned" baby. Their second child is a son, overweight and moody. What kind of dad will he make? What kind of sons will he raise? It will be two or three more years before the direction of the third child becomes obvious. The three small children are untrained, sadly lacking self-discipline like their older counterparts. How many families are there like this one? More than I care to acknowledge. Daddy is always gone, trying to make a living. Mom is always sick or tired, so the children are left to themselves. Do they not take seriously the Biblical statement *"A child left to himself bringeth his mother to shame (Prov. 29:15)?"* It takes more than birth to make a saint. It takes a new birth.

As I sit in the airport, waiting to board, I overhear a conversation. She looks like a homeschool mother, struggling with several unruly kids. She says to another passenger, "And how many children do you have?" Why did the question sound like a boast? The passenger says something I can't hear, and the mother responds in a sanctimonious tone, "Really! I have seven, so far." I look around and count. Yes, there are seven. The three-year-old is in the stroller yelling in a loud, angry, demanding voice, "Daddy! Daddy! Daddy! I want to be pushed right now! DADDY!" The shrill voice screeches on and on. But Daddy is trying to make ticket connections while struggling with the five-year-old, who is "having a very bad day." Perhaps he is tired from traveling. Mother is nursing the baby while another child quietly goes through someone else's belongings. The oldest children sit and stare at the TV. I want to stand up and apologize to those in the airport waiting room! "This woman knows not what she does." Instead, I put my head down and pretend I don't notice. I am so tired of pretending.

What am I trying to say? I am saying that I see Christian, homeschool families, dedicated to having large families, giving birth to children who will have a rat's existence, the same as that unwed mother, shacked up in that dump with no running water, heat, or furniture. There is no guarantee of salvation. Your children are not born with your convictions, certainly not your regenerated soul. They come into the world as empty vessels. The children of Christian parents are of the same flesh as those born in the hole. They are equally prone to an animal's existence of eating, drinking, demanding, commanding, taking and using. Their future is tied to the rest of the human race, unless you do something radical to alter their course. Home birth, homeschooling, not using birth control, modest dress, and making whole wheat bread are preferences not radical enough to save your children from the despair of the damned.

Having sons and daughters can be a temporal blessing. Raising children to be sons and daughters of God is a Divine calling. It requires an everyday, all-that-you-have commitment. Don't tell me how many you have birthed; tell me how many are walking in truth. "Well," you say, "they are all under seven years old." Then how many are walking in truth this very day? By example, are you raising them today to be saints of the Living God? It takes many todays to make a tomorrow. Children don't just naturally become better people. If at two years old they are pitching fits, then at seven they will be quietly refusing to obey simple commands, and at fourteen they will be like rats living to gratify their lusts.

The vast majority of people who seek our help seek it for their teenagers. They begin to reap what they have sown when their crop of children are somewhere between twelve and sixteen years old. When we make mention of the disobedience of the two- or seven-year-old, they are offended and think we are too picky. I want to shout, "Give me your unbroken vessels; you have already spoiled your teens with years of leaving them to themselves." Why do you think the younger five children will be any better than the two you have already raised?

Remember, your life speaks louder than your words. You can't blame them for not respecting your words when your attitude is repulsive. Who you are at home is whom you are inside. The contents of your carefully guarded soul will eventually spill out, and the children are always there to see it. Children are the first ones to spot a hypocrite and the first ones to want to flee from fraudulent, irate, religious parents. Have you caused God to stink in the nostrils of your children? It would have been far better for your children if you had never worn the religious cloak than to wear it with dishonor.

The needs of the Christian home are the needs of the church, of the nation, and the world. The world waits on the church to repent to its God, and the church waits on the families to live their profession. Families need parents to show the way of truth and holiness—not holiness of doing, but holiness of being, the holiness of love and mercy, of self-discipline and consistency.

You must train your children to be self-disciplined. But more than that, you must be living before your children a life so wonderfully different that they can only think of it as the presence and blessing of God. Only then will they hunger and thirst after righteousness instead of what the world has to offer. You can't talk, discipline, or spank children into sainthood. They must be drawn to desire to follow you into the kind of person you would desire them to be. It takes all of your energy, attention and concentration today and everyday to raise a child. Are you up to the task? Will you join me with a cry of pure longing: "Oh, God, I repent of all my selfishness and irritability. Teach me to walk with you in the paths of holiness. Take this child for your own. Cause this child to know you, to honor you, cause his life to be an example of your mercy and grace." And will you hear the Savior say, "Your job has just begun." ☺

Dear Pearls,

We have very much enjoyed your book, <u>To Train Up A Child</u>. We have 6 kids, 2-15 years old and wish we had had your book all along the way. We always tried to train instead of punish, but it is nice to have it in book form and to know we did a little bit right. People make comments to us to the tune of "if you had our kids to deal with...," like ours were born obeying, and we just dressed and fed our naturally adjusted, obedient kids.

Your book has helped us to see how much we give in to our 3-year-old. Our six children can each be characterized as: being indifferent, no emotions, affectionate, live wire, prissy, and a talker. They all need different care, but they all need the same switch. The Lord literally planted a mulberry tree in my flower garden, and we are supplied with switches most of the year. It is great how the Lord teaches us to train and discipline. Spank them and go on. We don't ground for 394 days or hold something over the kids for months, but I could probably write a book on the mistakes we've made. I have had 2 of your books—one I loaned out and will probably never see again. The other I gave to some friends expecting their first baby. Now I have none and could never be able to buy all that I could use.

Thanks, Michele

Potty Training

Dear Pearls,

Thank you so much for your ministry and faithfulness to God and His Word. I wanted to share with you a little about my friend Robin. I hope some day she will write her story for you. Her sixth child was born a few months ago with Down's Syndrome. As my daughter and I were visiting with her (after the birth) we happened to mention your book. She didn't have one, so we gave her ours. She read the chapter on potty training infants and started with her baby. I won't go into all the details (I don't know them all), but last month her tiny daughter had heart surgery in Cincinnati and ended up with 4 or 5 nurses watching her potty. They were amazed, and Robin left her copy of *To Train Up A Child* with one of the nurses! Henceforth, a larger order this time, as I so enjoy giving your books away.

Thank God my daughter, who is 20, knows the principles of child rearing from reading your book. It is never too early. I see such tragedy all around in families who have not trained their children.

May God bless you, Carolyn

Dear Precious Pearls,

You have transformed our household with <u>To Train Up A Child</u>. We have had such victory over years of wrong behavior, parent anger, and child disobedience. We have homeschooled for eight years. Our sons are 7, 10, and 17. You can't imagine what a burden has been lifted from me, especially now that I don't have to become angry, etc. Our youngest sons read the book to each other. Our 17-year-old loves it as well. I told him, "You were brought up wrong. Here is the right way." He has corrected himself in key ways through reading your book! Our church is eager to receive your book, and I have had an opportunity to testify to the Lord's work through reading your book. We are upholding you in prayer.

You broke heavy bondage for us all, and we are happier and more blessed for it!

In His Love, S.E.

Butterflies and Backdoors

With five children still at home, their friends come in like mosquitoes in Louisiana; you just try to ignore the buzz and hope they don't eat too much. I spend a lot of time in my office at the rear of the house. Its remoteness shuts out the noise. I especially try to coordinate my withdrawal with the arrival of a swarm. When I get ready to sleep at night, I just open the front door and stand by it until they all take leave. My wife says I am getting older. I think she is implying more than thinning hair and the senior citizen discounts I am increasingly offered. But I still have one weak spot.

The other day I was typing away, ignoring the recent arrivals. After a few minutes, when I had forgotten all about them, I heard the door behind me creak. I turned around and looked through the glass, but there was no one visible. Still the door continued to slowly creak open. Then I heard a cheerful little voice inquire, "Mack Peerle?" No, I haven't failed to spell my name correctly. That is the way Middle Tennessee hillbillies pronounce my name. You think that's funny; wait till you see what they do with yours. I again heard my Tennessee name as a little blond head peeped around the bottom corner of the door. She was not a mosquito; she was a butterfly. It was the most beautiful smile I have seen since I accepted my wife's proposal to marriage. I forgot about the Hypostatic Union, and said, "Here I am!" She came through my door like morning sunshine through the kitchen window. I returned her smile ten times over, ruffled her hair, and tossed her in the air, which is what she expected. We had a little chat, and then she found her way back to the noisy hum. I feel real important when I receive a guest of that caliber.

Now, beyond relating one of the great pleasures of life, that little visit would be of no significance to you unless you knew what occurred just two days earlier. My visitor, Amy, just turned two, has visited us on several occasions. They call it "baby-sitting." I call it "baby chasing." She is well above average in her self-control, but still has some rough spots. During the first few visits, I never attempted discipline. My youngest daughter, Shoshanna, had already gained her confidence and respect and does very well commanding her. I took those earlier visits as a time to gain her respect and devotion—to assure her of my delight and interest in her as a person.

On the visit before this welcomed intrusion, Amy ran in and out of the back door about ten times. The frequency, along with the cold air, became annoying. As she started out again, I commanded, "No, Amy, do not go out again." She continued to open the door and push by me. I applied a little resistance to the door as I repeated the command. She exerted all her force to open the door. Now at this point I could have forced the door shut. At six-foot-four and 240 pounds, all of it pure, aged muscle, I was quite capable of shutting the door. But to do so would not have taught her obedience, quite the  opposite. It would have taught her that she could do anything that does not meet with overpowering physical resistance. Forced to comply, she would not have practiced self-control. For the human will to function, circumstances must permit choice. So I allowed her to choose. She forced the door against the little resistance I offered and continued into the sunroom. One more door stood between her and the judgment seat. To make sure she understood, I gave one more command, "Amy, do not go outside." As she opened the outside door, I took off my belt and surprised my little butterfly with one swat across the calves. She shut the door and looked at me with shock and anger. Her scream was not just of pain, but of defiance.

Now if I had shoved her into the house and left it at that, she would still have failed to learn her lesson. Her will was not yet surrendered. The defiant scream testified that she was still in a resistant state of mind. She was protesting interference with her self-will. She must be caused to recognize the supremacy of government. Her soul depends on it. So I commanded, "Amy, stop crying." She screamed louder, so I gave her another forceful lick on the legs. She again screamed her defiance.

At this point, if I had become frustrated and shown anger in my expression or actions, it would have poisoned her soul. We would have become adversaries. I would have outwardly conquered, but she would have increased in her rebellion. Everyone hates a bully, and it becomes a matter of principle to resist him or her. Out of fear, one may surrender to a bully, but no one will ever respect the bully. Bullies are angry, self-willed, take offenses personally, exact their due in the pain of compliance, and maintain an attitude of "No one does this to me and gets away with it." Most parents bully their children.

Here I was with a screaming, defiant two-year-old standing there testing her strength of resolve against mine. I have 53 years of resolve, and it gets calmer every day. Again I gave her one lick on the legs and commanded, "Stop crying, now." She dried it up like an Arizona wind, then turned and voluntarily walked back into the living room. She was sniffling, but the defiance was all gone. She ran to a corner to sort out her feelings and I left her alone, as did everyone else. In less than five minutes, as I was walking through the house for some other purpose, a little curly headed, blond butterfly flitted across the room and lunged into my arms. Her smile was genuine and her greeting was spontaneous. The former confrontation had not left her feeling isolated. Her spirit was free. A properly administered spanking does not break fellowship.

About two hours later I was in my bedroom reading, when I again heard the door being pushed open. "Mack Peerle, cun I'go ootsidd?" The kids had all gone out on the front porch to attend to the chicken they were cooking on the grill. She was the only one left inside, but she had learned her lesson. I said, "Sure, Amy, you can go out with the others." She gave me a grateful smile and ran out the front door.

When she left that day, I had not seen any additional signs of rebellion, but I did wonder how she would be when she came to the house again. So, several days later, when the door creaked open and I saw that Amy had come to share smiles with me, I appreciated her parents, and I was thankful that my mother and father taught me how to train up a child. ☺

The Reconciler

When "The Reconciler" left this planet, He committed unto His disciples the *ministry of reconciliation*. The church exists not as a celebration of our past reconciliation, but as an army of reconcilers. A church that is not reproducing itself is as useless as a fruit tree bearing no fruit. The church was not meant to be a well-proportioned ornament—providing shade for its own branches; it is intended that it should sacrifice its limbs to the weight of excess fruit.

We train our children, not that they might rise in the world, but that they might descend into the place of need to deliver captives. The standard by which one measures success in this life will be viewed with sorrow and disdain in the next. The ultimate goal of the church and of the family is to reach the world with the good news of Christ. ☺

Dear Mike and Debi,

Thank you so much for your ministry. I first learned about your book from an ad in <u>Teaching Home</u>. It sounded too good to be true (I am usually very skeptical about these kinds of things)! I was pleasantly surprised to find that your claims were not unfounded and that your methods (taken straight from Proverbs) worked miracles. At that time, my husband as a Navy officer was gone about 80% of the time. I survived the 6-month deployment of his ship alone with 4 small children in large part because of your book. It was unfortunate that he missed the transition. He came back expecting the same old order and found that things had changed radically. Now, two years later, I can see that he is still scratching his head. Your book not only transformed me, it transformed the children. I am just glad that my husband can come home in the evening and enjoy the results of a relatively peaceful home, and children who are respectful and obedient. I am looking forward to the close, loving relationship I know I will enjoy with my toddler, and soon after, the other will follow. Thanks for sharing your "uncommon common sense."

A.C.

"What Daddy Doesn't Know Won't Hurt Him"

By Debi

Linda, who is just three years old, loves to go to Grandma's house. The first thing she does when she runs through the door is to ask for candy. Daddy won't let her eat candy, but Mama doesn't see anything wrong with it. Linda knows Mama and Daddy have differences of opinion about things. Daddy says "no" about a lot of things, but Mama is more fun. She knows it is not really bad, for she just laughs and says, "Daddy doesn't need to know; what he doesn't know won't hurt him." Linda heard her mama tell Grandma this, so Grandma lets the little girls eat candy at her house. Grandma says she ate candy when she was young and it didn't hurt her. And Grandma says she "wouldn't want to deprive her granddaughter of a good old American tradition. There are some things daddies just don't know anything about."

Linda loves her daddy. He likes to take her with him when he goes places, and there is nothing Linda likes better. Linda is such a good little girl; everyone says so. She is so obedient and kind to others. She would never dare pitch a fit. Everyone should be so blessed, having a little darling like Linda.

But a dangerous seed has already sprouted in Linda. Its roots have begun to grow, spreading its ugly, entwining, choking tentacles around the very soul of this precious child. Mama planted that seed with her laughter; she waters those roots with her deceit; she fertilizes that unseen plant with her carelessness concerning Daddy's wishes. Mama is cultivating the plant that one day will strangle the truth from Linda's heart and life. Mama thinks, "What Daddy doesn't know won't hurt him," but someday it will break his heart. Little girls get to be big girls with bigger issues than eating sweets. Other things get to be "sweeter." When the day comes that Mama and Daddy discover Linda is keeping secrets from both of them, thinking that they are just "old fashioned, and wouldn't understand," no one will laugh, not even Grandma. But then Linda says to her friends, "What they don't know won't hurt them." Somebody lied. It's hurting them—deeper than anything ever has. ☺

More Potty Training

Dear Michael and Debi,

Thank you so much for all your articles on "Potty Untraining." We've just tried it out with our 3rd child. Our <u>newborn</u> successfully "oopsied" on his first try on the toilet at only 4 weeks old. He's 7 weeks old now and we've only had to wash 2 oopsied diapers, and one was Mama's fault. He oopsies 5 or 6 times each day. You can imagine how happy this mama is, especially since we use cloth diapers. When we excitedly shared this news with my husband's folks back in Holland, they, of course, did not believe it. While we were trying to explain, we realized that the root form of the Dutch word for diaper literally means, "lazy."

Also, an interesting side note: our 30-month-old had not "oopsied" on the pot despite all our best efforts to encourage him...until he saw his baby brother do it. Thanks for all the clean laundry!

Nap Family

Mike Responds

Dear Naps,

Your letter was refreshing and fun. We have received letters where parents told us that we lost credibility by making such absurd claims about potty training infants. Americans and Europeans, are going through a renaissance of the Dark Ages in family and childcare. Thank God for many bold enough to break out of the bondage.

Mike

Mr. and Mrs. Pearl,

I was blessed to receive your book as a gift. It has been of great encouragement to my husband and me. Nothing for us was working; our girls were becoming defiant and terrified of us. But praise God for you and this book for truly giving us hope in regaining our girls and training them properly.

Roci

The Parental Root

A mother wrote this letter to us. It is so terribly typical, we feel compelled to answer it plainly. As you read it, think of yourself as the counselor and take note of your own responses. Do you sympathize with her plight? Are you in similar circumstances? What would you tell her to do?

After a paragraph of complimentary introduction, she gets down to the issue:

> Now I will convey to you the complications I seem to have with rearing my three children.

> I praise our Lord for a wonderful Christian home. But with the struggles of each day, the varying differences between my husband and I seem to intensify with the delicate process of rearing our three children. They are ages 10, 6 1/2, & 4. As a result of my husband becoming a true and genuinely active Christian after the age of 36, he has contrarily maintained a somewhat conflicting and contradictory viewpoint in specific relation to the more liberal attitude toward training and disciplining our children. This obviously creates a greater difficulty to uphold a truly consistent pattern of discipline. I believe godly principles dictate a parental enforcement and reinforcement of obedience to God and parents.

> I am interested in your answer to one specific area of dispute. My husband contends that a 10-year-old little girl is "too big" to spank, but I disagree. Could you please clarify this according to your principles of understanding?

> Another specific concern might be with regard to negative attitudes from children at the time of completing an instruction to do household chores or daily routines. Please present your viewpoint on this issue. Thanks so much for the godly instruction you provide. May God richly bless your ministries as well as you and your family.

> Sincerely, Vastly Conservative Mother of 3

Thanks for your plain letter. I will be equally plain in my answer. You have described your family problems from your one-sided perspective, which is the way we usually hear the details of a conflict. From many years of counseling I have learned to never take at face value the interpretation of just one member of a controversy. And with no more than the contents of just one letter, it is difficult to be certain in my interpretation of the situation, but to answer, it is necessary to make some assumptions. If there were just 100 questions with 100 answers, I could match the answer with the question. Like your question as to whether or not it is appropriate to spank a 10 year old girl: There is no one right answer that covers all circumstances. Fathers usually cease spanking girls at an earlier age than do mothers. Perhaps for him, she is too old; for you, maybe an occasional spanking is still in order. It differs with the child and the relationship you maintain with him or her. Under normal conditions, where training started sooner, a ten-year-old would not need spanking. You better get the job done in a hurry; she will likely be too old for a spanking by the time she is twelve.

As to your question regarding the bad attitude of children faced with unpleasant commands, again, there is not a single answer that covers all situations. I cannot say that all children with bad attitudes should be spanked until they smile, or given double workloads until they are thankful, etc. We have offered several practical solutions to this issue in this book as well as in *No Greater Joy, Volumes One* and *Two*. The main thing is to never allow the child's attitude to control your expectations, unless it is to cause you to demand more.

Understand me. Family is first a matter of relationships, not techniques and appropriate responses. If you are running a correctional facility with inmates, you could spell out the proper penalty and response to a given infraction of the rules, and by being consistent you could maintain discipline and order. But our goal in parenting is to train a soul into godliness, not just gain compliance.

From the child's perspective, training is better instituted through emulation rather than capitulation. If we lose the child's heart, we have lost the battle before we even know what the issues are. The attitude of parents, the mother in particular, is the fountain from which flows all family relationships—Mother is the morale of the family. Therefore, as counselors, until we have dealt with parental attitudes we are wasting our time. A technique that is right for one person can be wrong for another, when it is dished out with the wrong attitude. A rod can heal or destroy. A rebuke can bring repentance or communicate rejection. A warning can turn the heart of the child before it gets out of hand or it can produce rebellion. There is no technique or appropriate response that can conceal a parent's heart and produce fruit different from the parental root.

To answer your questions—the questions of any parent where conflict is the issue—I must address the attitude of the parent; I must make some bold assumptions. I am limited to generalizations, limited to the many personal experiences I have had in hearing questions phrased and then digging deeper until I could attach a disposition to them. It helps greatly to look into the eyes and read body language, but I must know you through your words.

The general content of your letter assumes that the fault in your home is your husband's. Before you begin to discuss the issues, you say the right words: "praise the Lord for a wonderful Christian home," and for a "true and genuinely active Christian husband." Those statements are not consistent with that which follows, for in reference to your husband, you speak of, "varying differences between my husband and I seem to intensify." He has "contrarily maintained...conflicting and contradictory viewpoint," with an attitude that is "more liberal" than your own. Your husband creates a "greater difficulty." You have "one specific area of dispute" with him. Your husband "contends," and you "disagree." If this is a "wonderful Christian home" don't expect any converts.

You must understand, we are all possessed with an inordinate drive to control. That one is seeking to control others in the realm of religion does not sanctify the selfish drive. If the Devil was limited to imparting just one vice, I suspect he would choose a religious controlling spirit. The drive to dominate has worked more evil in the world than any other factor. Homes are destroyed and children are scarred, not by bad training techniques or by one member of the family that is "too liberal," but by two people competing for domination. The children can survive a little liberality. They can survive too few or too many spankings, but the conflict that arises between two parents seeking to control each other, even for the greater good, creates a caustic atmosphere that rots the souls of their children.

It is a great beginning to accept the reality that there is only one person in the world we can control—ourselves. And self-control is a lifetime challenge, managed only through the Lord Jesus Christ. To control others is an elusive sweetness reserved for the violent and the mesmerizing cultist. But there is hardly a marriage that is not bleeding from attempts to control and dominate. The mother cuts the father, as you have done in this letter; the father cuts the mother, and the children bleed. They ask me for medicine to give the children to stop the bleeding, and when I tell the parents that they are the ones who need to take the medicine, they are sure I am directing my advice to the other partner, the one that will not cooperate.

Your letter implies: you cannot be a good wife and mother, and you cannot train your children, because your husband will not cooperate. Understand this. You cannot wait until the world is a good place before you become good. You cannot wait until the church is revived to experience your own revival. And you cannot wait until your spouse is right before you do right. You must be the kind of person God requires, despite the condition of your spouse. Your spouse is outside the limits of your control. Accept that and go forward, or stop here and dig in your heels, which will create a grave for your children. If you make your husband's compliance a condition to the success of your parenting, you have already lost the battle. Children can survive inconsistency, but they will never survive dissension and tension.

I am not using hyperbole when I say your children would be in a better condition if you were as "liberal" as your husband, believed exactly as he does, and the two of you were joyously in sync at his lower level of "enforcement." They would grow up with sloppy habits, possibly a bit lazy, probably lack a high measure of self-control, but they would be emotionally secure. They would feel loved, valued, and, most importantly of all, they would not be bitter and rebellious, as they will being raised in a home filled with parental conflict. You can minister life to your children by providing an atmosphere that says you are absolutely delighted with your husband, but you only minister death if they feel you are in disagreement with him. By your rejection of your husband—the ultimate authority in the home—you erode the very concept of authority in the minds of your children. Regardless of your words, you are training them in rebellion.

This concept is the most important training principle I can give you, and it is the most common need. It reminds me of an experience I had when I was about ten years old. My parents left my eight-year-old brother and me at home. We were ordered to do the dishes, after which we could split an entire chocolate pie. I loved chocolate pie. To be able to split a whole chocolate pie into two equal pieces and eat half by myself was joy beyond description. As we washed the dishes we began to argue over who was going to cut the pie. Neither of us trusted the other to be fair in dividing it. I was two years older and was obviously more qualified to enforce my broadly experienced will. But my brother was equally determined to make sure justice was accomplished. When the last dish was put away, we both rushed to the table. I pulled the pie over to make the cut. He pulled it back his way. We struggled until the pie landed upside down on the dirty kitchen floor. I can still feel the total sense of loss, seeing that beautiful chocolate pie splattered out in a two foot circle, the cat lapping at the edges. It was a total loss. Of course it was his fault for not appreciating my judgment. But he thought it was my fault for enforcing my will. When our parents came home and heard our complaints, they only laughed, saying something about "hoping we had learned our lesson." I'm sure he didn't. That was 43 years ago and still he has not repented. Oh well, he just wouldn't listen to sound advice.

Now, my slightly embellished story is certainly funny today; from time to time when we get together we laugh over it. But I hope you were able to interpret my little parable. Parents who struggle over how to raise the kids, end up spilling the whole pie. It would be better to resign yourself to eating a smaller piece of pie, no matter the cost to your pride, than to demand your rights and end up standing over the mess. Is blame so sweet that you would risk the pie just to see that he doesn't get away with anything? You say, "But it is different; I am fighting for the right for my kids to eat pie." A big piece of pie eaten in tension may cause indigestion or regurgitation. A little piece eaten in peace, with thankfulness, is the good life.

I have often said, "If you find that your expectations of your spouse or your children are so high that you are angry at them for failing to comply, it is far better to lower your expectations to your smiling threshold than to scowl at them from your high perch." We are not asking you to compromise truth, but to resign as policeman of that truth. We are not asking you to lay aside your convictions, but to lay aside the conviction that you are duty bound to pass those convictions on to your husband, and that he should be obliged to follow your lead. Truth, love, discipline, justice, joy, and obedience are not well supported by criticism, blame, anger, and accusation.

You are not responsible for the actions of your husband. If he is truly less capable than you are, demonstrate your expertise by training your children in such a way that they never suspect there is any conflict. They may know that you are tougher and absolutely consistent, but they will suppose that such is just normal. "Daddy and Mama love each other dearly. He lets us get away with more than she does, but we know that when he is not around we had better walk the line."

Mother, you spend far more time with your little ones than he does. In most homes, the mother is responsible for more than 80% of the training time, and the father for less than 20%. If you do your job right, he will not be able to undo it in the evening, unless you set up a tension that causes the children to lose respect for both of you and for authority in general. In which case, they will rebel against you, knowing that they are working two opposing sides. When parents are not known to be in perfect agreement, do not present a unified command, in the minds of the children it leaves an authority vacuum, and the kids will step in to fill that vacuum. You, Mother, are the only one who can communicate the concept that there is divided authority. The children will never interpret the differences between the liberal father and the strict mother as divided command unless you communicate that through open challenge in their presence or through slights you make when he is not present.

I know what you are thinking: "But I cannot just give up and resign my children to what I know is going to be very bad training. They are too important to allow my husband to spoil them." You are still assuming that you can fight a battle with your husband and change him. You are still convinced that if you just push harder and demand more, he will eventually see the error of his way and follow you in your greater wisdom. Yea, and if it happens, it will be the first time in the history of the world that a husband has bowed to pressure from his wife and matured as a result. No man ever crawled out from under the burden his wife placed on him to become a better man. Such is the illusion of a controlling spirit. I am not commending the male ego; I am stating reality. Flow with it and prosper, or resist it and die with the satisfaction that it was your husband that destroyed your family—you stood on your principles.

If parents withhold affection from a child on the condition that he deserves it, he will never seek affection from his parents, and will eventually reach a place where he will resent affection and reject it if they try to give it. Likewise, if a husband withholds love from his wife on the condition that she honor him, she will dishonor him with the zeal of a fanatic. And she will deliberately make him aware of those whom she does honor, just to show him what he is missing. And so it is that if a woman withholds honor from her husband on the condition that he become honorable, he may become honorable for others, but he will never become honorable for her. If you fail to take into account the reverse psychology of a fallen, perverted race, you are building on fanciful imaginations.

It seems like a hopeless cycle. And it is, without a miracle. Just look at society around you. Until someone lays his own life down, his own ambitions, his own edification, his rights, his pride, and gives without regard to return, in short, until someone loves as Christ loved, there will be no healing, no growth, no proper child training. The alternative is to stand your ground and wait for him to pull his share, which means the load will never get delivered. Or you can pull the load for the both of you, and take no thought of it. Never remind him; never complain; know it is your joy to be the kind of person God requires you to be, even if the whole world decides to ride in your wagon. If you do not feel sufficient to the task, welcome to the Christian life. The choice is yours. You can choose for only one person, and it is not your husband. ☺

Getting in Tune

Just this week, I heard a mother tell with amusement how her son had announced that he was going to be a musician—a guitarist. For several weeks, while he searched for and purchased just the right guitar, he told all his friends of his great future as a guitarist. Eventually, a friend of the family came over and showed him how to form just three basic cords in the key of C. When the young man tried it, he found that it "hurt" his fingers. He also found that his wrist got tired from strumming. And it didn't sound at all as if his music would make it to the charts. His vision of fame and glory quickly faded. He still has his guitar. It sits in a corner, not tuned—he never learned how. His fingers don't hurt anymore, and he never mentions his former dreams.

Just a few days ago, I observed a young mother interacting with her first child. Not too long ago she was planning her wedding and talking about her coming marriage and the family she would raise. Having been exposed to much teaching and some good examples on child training, she was often heard discussing how she was going to have happy, obedient children. "It's just terrible what they let that child get away with," she would say.

She is now married and has a child. Recently, I heard someone say of her and her husband, "It's just terrible what they let that child get away with." She is a very sweet mother—the sweetest of all. She's protective and loving, often seen reassuring her little girl. She started out with the highest expectations for her family, but she found that it hurts to practice training your children. It takes time, energy, emotion, and, like guitar playing, you sometimes have to sacrifice your tenderness for toughness. That can hurt.

Today this mother is known to have "the most spoiled child I have ever seen." She is a fine person, a good Christian, a good wife, and a "good mother." But she will never play the guitar, and her girl will never "walk in the way she should go." When she is encouraged or counseled, she just doesn't get it.

"Oh, she'll grow out of it," she says. "She's just not like other kids. All kids are different you know." The father explains his child by laughing and saying, "It is one thing to talk about training; it is something else to do it." He is implying that it is an unlikely task, as if he were being asked to teach her to read by age three. The lightness with which he discusses his whining, demanding daughter indicates that he puts it in the same category with learning to ride a bicycle—she is late, but she will catch up. Late child training is somewhat like being late in putting the milk in the refrigerator.

Just two days ago, while answering child training questions over a radio talk show, I was asked the same question I have been asked a thousand times: "If you have a friend who has read your books and agrees with everything you say, yet it makes no change in their family—they go on doing it the same old way—how do you help them?" I gave the same answer, "I can't." There is one thing a parent must bring to the process of instruction in child training—a mental state—a vision, fortitude, determination, expectation. If old-fashioned grit is missing, you can't learn to play the guitar, nor can you tune your children. Nothing happens just because you talk about it or because you read a book. Establishing priorities and following through on commitments is essential to accomplish any worthy end. You either pay the price to train, or later you pay the bigger price for having not trained. ☺

Dear Michael and Debi

My husband and I had pretty much reached the end of our resources to train and discipline our two children. Then last Wednesday night the tension came to a head, and basically my husband and I turned on each other. It was awful.

That night I prayed, "Lord, I have no idea what to do—PLEASE help us—we're drowning!" The very next day a friend came by for lunch. During the course of our visit, she said, "I brought by a couple of books—I thought they were pretty good." Later that day, I began to read *To Train Up a Child*, and I read excerpts out loud to my husband. We both quickly realized that God had provided the solution to our problem. He blessed so much—my husband doesn't usually read books, but he took that one and read it before I did. We were both amazed and rejoiced at the answer to our prayer! In just a day we saw a difference in our children. Through reading your material, God opened our eyes to the awesome responsibility of parenting. We don't want to be reactive parents anymore.

Gratefully, S. & K. M.

Rodless Training?

I just hung up the phone after talking with a pastor concerning a new member in his church. This single mother had been hopelessly bound in drugs and immorality, living a life of sin and degradation. The state had removed the children from her home. For two years they were passed around from institution to temporary residence, to institution, and back again. This mother, forsaken by all but the predators who sought to consume the scared flesh that remained, was lost—alone, wasted, hopeless. *"But God...(Eph. 2:4)."* Then someone told her about the forgiveness that was purchased by the blood of Jesus. In a moment's time, without the aid of religious ritual or

practiced instruction, she was translated from the kingdom of darkness into the kingdom of God's dear Son (Col. 1:13). It is called the new birth and is the only door to heaven (John 3). The state quickly recognized that she was not the same person whose lifestyle had necessitated the removal of her children. The children were sent home to their new mother. But when she sought to begin a new life with her children, she found they were as inmates released from captivity, monsters of contention and rebellion. Children that start life in a government institution often end up in one.

The pastor related the dilemma. He had given her our book, but when she attempted to implement the things she learned, she realized that she was setting herself up to lose the children back to the state. For when she spanked them, they would scream, "Please don't whip me!" She is still on probation and must receive visits from social workers. If a child was to reveal that he was being spanked, the children would be immediately removed and placed back in a soulless institution. There they would not be bruised on the outside, but they would continue to rot from the inside.

So the pastor's question was, "Is there a way to train children if you are prevented from Biblical application of the rod?" The Bible says, *"Foolishness is bound in the heart of a child; but the rod of correction shall drive it far from him (Prov. 22:15)."*

"Withhold not correction from the child: for if thou beatest him with the rod, he shall not die. Thou shalt beat him with the rod, and shalt deliver his soul from hell (Prov. 23:13-14)."

"The rod and reproof give wisdom: but a child left to himself bringeth his mother to shame (Prov. 29:15)."

This question has been asked in more than one way. It is a common situation. One parent absolutely stands against use of the rod, and so it could not be employed effectively. Can the other parent still train the children? If you are a foster parent, you are forbidden to use the rod. Perhaps you are host to your grandchildren and not allowed to spank them. Maybe you are often in charge of the neighbor's kids. Likewise, you are limited if you are a worker in a daycare or if you are a schoolteacher.

The question is, "If I am in a position where I cannot use the rod, am I already doomed to failure, or is there still hope? Can children be trained without use of the rod?" Absolutely! But they cannot be absolutely trained. Proper application of the rod is indispensable to communicating the divine principle of retributive justice, but any child, military man, employee, the neighbor's kid, your dog, cat, the birds in your yard, or the fish in the river can be trained through manipulating their relationship to their environment. Any creature that is self-motivated and has likes and dislikes can be trained if you are in a position to reward or deny any pleasure or need. Where humans are concerned, you have the added tools of reason, moral persuasion, social persuasion, and conscience. Where it concerns those that are close to you, that is, they depend upon your fellowship for their mental satisfaction, you have the additional tools of persuasion and example.

If you are seeking to avoid the rod because you are an emotional coward, or because you are a product of contemporary philosophy, then not obeying God in this matter should not be considered an option. The Word of God teaches us the best method of child training, and proper use of the rod is a part of that program. Furthermore, if you abstain from use of the rod because you believe there is a better way, then you have revealed a fundamental flaw in your thinking that will leave a giant hole in any method you adopt. In other words, a person who understands the value and principle of the rod, but is somehow prevented from using it, will carry those valuable principles over into rodless training and so reap some of the benefits. Whereas the person that does not believe in use of the rod is so flawed in his understanding of human nature and life in general that no technique will be entirely effective for him.

So if circumstances beyond your control prevent you from doing as God commands, you are not without tools. There are still plenty of options available to you. You can do a relatively good job of training if you are consistent and recognize the nature of your limitations. You will have to lean more heavily on alternatives that tend toward accomplishing the same end.

Here is a single mother with chaotic children whom she must train without the assistance of the ultimate force—pain. She tells them to do something, and they immediately seek to do the opposite. She invites them to the table, and they tarry or declare that they are not hungry. Thirty minutes later they are demanding something sweet. When she refuses, they begin to cry and beg. When she tells them to stop, they scream. Then they start fighting between themselves. When she tries to interfere, they turn on her in violence. Their favorite word is "no" spoken with defiance. They will say "no" even when they would actually like to comply, just to express their autonomy.

Let's take it further so as to be relevant to a larger audience. If she were to spank them, they would react by screaming and fighting her. They would pull away, try to grab the switch, scream "No," and go completely hysterical. She could not spank them until they yielded, unless she spanked them into physical exhaustion, which of course would be counterproductive. In short, in her attempt to build a relationship with them, at this early stage, spanking would not likely be profitable anyway. You may be thinking, "My children have always been in a secure environment and they act just like that."

The foremost need in child training, the ground on which all positive guidance occurs, is the relationship of child to parent. Her children are doubtlessly in an adversarial frame of mind. It is not just that they seek to put forward their own agenda, but that they actually seek to sabotage hers. It is vain to make her will clear, because they have already decided to resist all control. A rebel is not so concerned with doing his own thing as he is in not doing the will of another. He dedicates himself to publicly demonstrating that he is not in subjection to any authority. It is his agenda to rebel, to prove his independence and lack of respect.

Now we who are not emotionally involved are inclined to see the situation from the child's point of view. The poor children have been emotionally deprived and abused. It is not their fault that they were jerked up and passed around like a piece of rental equipment. They are hostile because they have never known love and security. They have never had anyone they could trust to always be there. They are products of the adults surrounding them.

However, if we now handle them under our own shadow of guilt and sympathy, they will be further ruined. If our understanding of their plight causes us to sympathize, we will only authenticate their hostilities. You must remember, children raised under the best of circumstances, in a home of love and security, are nonetheless inclined to selfish domination and independent action against the rule of law. If a child is "left to himself" he does not grow up beautiful, he grows up to be a little devil and will *"bring his mother to shame (Prov. 29:15)."* Her children are what they are because of neglect, but they are only being themselves. It is not a matter of just bad habits; it is now a case of bad character—yes, even at two years old.

But we are not going to blame the children, we are going to train them—however difficult, and without the use of the rod. We may not achieve as high results, but if we are wise and consistent, others will brag on "what good kids" we have.

In our first book on child training, we talked about "tying strings." The first step in all child training, the foundation stone that must be continually renewed, is fellowship between parent and child. In 99% of all homes, children are in an adversarial state of mind most of the time. The first step, the step without which all other attempts are in vain, is to establish mutual ties of respect and honor. Unless the children can trust their parents with the handling of their souls, they will not make themselves vulnerable. It is the same with you, is it not? Children must be brought to the place where they want to please their parents. Until children value the approval of their parents more than the lure of any indulgence, there is no foundation for training.

Fear of punishment is not sufficient to make children compliant; it will certainly not remove their adversarial mentality. When parents get to the place where they are relying on threats alone, they have totally lost fellowship and are functioning as the IRS. Threats might get outward compliance but never the heart—quite the opposite.

So there is nothing that prevents this mother from taking the first step in child training—establish a relationship of trust and respect. How is this done? Enjoy the children and cause them to enjoy you. Don't ask anything of them that is not absolutely necessary to the stability of the home, give them something they want—not selfish demands, just ignore those. Give them your time, your attention, your laugh, your approval, your touch, hugs, reading, silly funnies; roll on the carpet or out in the yard, push them in the swing, or pull them in the wagon. But most of all let them bask in your smile until they need it like they need their next breath. Cause them to feed on your fellowship, to relax until they are sure you care only for their good, that you live to enjoy their company and would not be happy without them. Do this and you will have achieved what most Christian homes are missing.

When you first begin to mend a broken relationship, or build one that never existed, you will have to do what friends do–ignore problem areas, absorb ugliness–for "they know not what they do." If they begin to trust you, and you strike at them, physically or verbally, they will withdraw, and it will take longer to draw them into the open again. You can stand firm on issues; just make sure that you are always relaxed and calm in your responses. If you have to reject an action, never communicate rejection of them as a person. The worse thing you can do in this attempt to rebuild the relationship is to develop critical feelings toward them and to become short and abusive in your language or attitude. They will shut you out like shutting the barn door on a winter storm. You can wipe out everything by having a condemning attitude.

Your reach as a disciplinarian cannot exceed the limits of your fellowship with the child. Rebuke must be delivered in an atmosphere of trust and respect. If you have lost the child's heart, then the child will have lost the heart to please you. If the child is not in agreement to pull with you, it is vain to try to harness him to your rules. The occasional rebuke must be the exception to a constant sharing of positive experiences. When rebuke and chastisement are strung along on a thread of long silences, punctuated by beads of unpleasantries, it will only strangle the relationship, not beautify the child's soul.

The other day my daughters took in a younger girl who was a product of the federal school, a working mother, and an insensitive father—in that order. She was at that age just before puberty when it is easy to be misunderstood and confused. The child had been swept along in the sexless society of the federal system. She was not feminine or lovely in demeanor. My girls spent the day treating her as another "lady." Toward the end of the day, when it was near time for her father to pick her up, they got her dressed in a long flowing dress. You could tell that at first it was an embarrassment to her to appear so vulnerable, so feminine, but she soon began to enjoy it. She started carrying herself differently. The affected gawkiness disappeared. She smiled with a blush and gracefully swept around the room. Soon her father came into the room. You could tell that she was pleased with herself and was expecting his approval. My daughters presented her to him as if she were a newly dressed bride, exclaiming how nice she looked in a dress. He blurted, "Yeah, I have been telling her she would look better in dresses. She just wears those old pants. The kids these days...." Her countenance fell and her shoulders hardened into the reserved condition she had displayed hours earlier. It was obvious to her that rather than her father being pleased with her, he was pleased with himself that she had justified what he "had been saying all along." On such small threads do our children hang. She had attempted to take a new course, one that could have made a great difference in her life, but his preoccupation with himself had shut the door in her face. He was not mean or cruel or angry—just insensitive, absorbed with his own performance, perhaps carrying latent irritation at having been ignored so long. He had a chance to join hearts with her, but he missed it.

Can you see that in such simple, day to day matters hangs all of child training? Until we tie strings of fellowship, all else is vain, even harmful. If you would train your children, and you are prevented from using the rod, you still have at your disposal a tool that most of my readers have never effectively employed—continuous fellowship with their child. If you can create an atmosphere of trust and goodwill, you will greatly reduce the need to spank the small child, and nearly eliminate the need in children eight or older.

After you have established fellowship with your child, the next step in training is to gain his respect as a person of principle. Your child must know that you answer to, and act as representative of, a rule of law that is higher than your own personal preference. You have boundaries that you adhere to, and expect him to do likewise. By reverencing boundaries in your own life, you communicate that there is a Lawgiver higher than your own feelings and impulses. If the child is made to feel that he must obey you only because you are bigger or tougher, or because you have control of the resources, then your influence will extend only until he is big enough to rebel without severe consequences. But if the child treasures your fellowship and wants to please you, and on top of that, the child wants to please the God that you please, then you have a solid foundation for training. The only battle left is the child's flesh.

Many parents have found, all too late, that religious instruction given in the context of permissiveness works to produce atheists and infidels rather than Christians. I personally know many families that took their children to church and talked spirituality, while indulging the flesh in food and pleasure, and indulging the soul in irritability and pettiness, with the result that their children grew up to resemble sons and daughters of Baal rather than children of a holy God. Children dragged through that kind of confusion are far harder to reach with the truth of Christ than are the abused and abusing sons and daughters of prostitutes and dope peddlers. I know whereof I speak. Besides dealing with hundreds of such cases, some of my own relatives serve as the best examples.

So, on a foundation of fellowship and respect for God, the Lawgiver, you are ready to deal with that indomitable enemy of all the sons of Adam—the flesh. Even when your child wants to please you and wants to please God, he is going to feel the constant pull of the desires of the flesh. *"The flesh lusteth against the spirit and the spirit against the flesh, and these are contrary the one to the other so that [your child] cannot do the things that he would (Gal. 5:17)."* Here is where the mechanics of training are inaugurated. Your young child is composed of two opposing elements—elements that were in harmony before the fall of Adam—the flesh and the spirit. The spirit is that inner man, the soulish self. The flesh is that material biological conglomerate of tissue, bone, and blood, that is endowed with passion and drives.

The spirit can receive instruction and make decisions based on values, whereas the flesh is indifferent to good and evil. Like any animal or plant, the flesh seeks survival and propagation. It battles within, seeking to maintain a stability that promotes health, and it strives without, seeking zones of comfort and pleasure. The body has no built-in governor that predetermines moderation or sets limits. It would eat what tastes good, and it would eat it now. It would rest rather than work and take rather than give. The flesh cares not how it affects others or what the long-range consequences might be. The flesh neither knows nor cares that present actions will result in cavities, obesity, colon cancer, heart disease, or venereal disease; it just pursues the line of immediate pleasure. Where there is not an active, mature, trained, and disciplined mind exercising control, the body is a self-destructive fungus.

The bottom line you must recognize is that the infant is born with all of the passions of flesh but with no capacity for self-restraint. Your three-year-old has active bodily drives, but no understanding or will to moderation and self-restraint. The child will be in his early to middle teens before he can function so as to be self motivated to the point of subjecting his flesh to his spirit. You can have a child with a submissive heart, but he cannot exercise his mind to self-restraint.

Herein is the parental responsibility: While your child is in the process of maturing, before he can govern himself, it is your responsibility to function as his spirit, as his governor. You will act as his conscience, his sensor, advisor, instructor, chastiser, rebuker. <u>You will say "no" to his flesh when he cannot</u>. You will be ever alert, vigilant, on guard to detect any uprising of flesh. You will strengthen his resolve to stand by the rule of law and deny the flesh. You will spot laziness and lead him in an attack against it. You will spot selfishness and see that it is not gratified. In short, you will never allow it to be a pleasing experience to indulge the flesh. He will be caused to find rest and peace in one path only—the path of holiness and self-discipline. Your job is to make all evil counterproductive and unrewarding and to make all righteousness and discipline to be delightful and joyous.

At this point, the parent would have the rod as an enforcer against the monster of flesh. When the flesh runs away with the spirit and captivates the will, when the child turns on you like an angry dog and refuses to give ground, the rod can restore his respect for your authority. It is your final tool against the power of the flesh to commit mutiny and take the will captive.

But our subject is: "What can you do if you are denied that ultimate power to subdue the flesh?" You can fully apply all of the above measures so that you do not come to that place where the rod is necessary. Yet, we must face the obvious truth that no parent is going to create a net of training so tight that the kids don't occasionally slip through. There will be times when a spanking is appropriate. But you are prevented! Then use your power as the caretaker and dispenser of all privileges and responsibilities to make his actions totally counterproductive. If you can't spank the flesh, starve it with an embargo. Stand your ground and do not let the little fellow find satisfaction in his pursuits. Stay on duty, demanding obedience until he surrenders his will to your persistence. If there is a way to deny him access to some means of indulgence that relates to the offense, then by all means, as governor of the island on which he lives, deny him normal privileges until he complies.

The one—most important—principle is to never allow his rebellion to be successful. Always win the contest. You can do this because of your position as banker, cook, house cleaner, playtime supervisor, work detail manager, etc. Stand your ground. If you develop a reputation as a winner of conflicts, you will be home free. If you develop a reputation as a vacillating wimp that whines and complains about how you are treated, he will run over you like a discarded aluminum can. The key is to win. Always win. Stand by your demands. Be just. Be reasonable. Be consistent. Be tough. Be there all the time, ever in his face, loving, laughing, smiling, and demanding compliance as foreman of the home.

Without use of the rod, you will be handicapped but not crippled. You won't do as good of a job as you could have done, but with determination and vigilance, you can do a better job than 99% of the other Christian parents who have full freedom to use the rod. ☺

Dear Pearls,

A while back, I wrote to you about my 2-year-old daughter who struggled with getting her hair washed and rinsed. You replied a while ago, and I wanted to thank you for taking the time to share with me your daughter's success with Jane! I followed suit and had dramatic results. I was a bit exhausted by all the enthusiasm I displayed when I poured water over my own head, but the effort paid off. My daughter struggled a bit, but our first time obedience training came in handy when I explained that this was not a cry-time, but a happy-time. She swallowed her sorrow and tried her best to smile as I sang about how fun it was to get water poured over your head. I discovered she really doesn't like water in her ears, so we made another game of plugging her ears with her fingers! I wish I had a video camera...Mom with soaking wet hair herself, a 2-year-old with fingers in her ears, and poorly written lyrics being sung out of tune about how fun it is to get your hair wet. Please thank your daughter Shoshanna for me! Sincerely trying to learn.

Thanks, Jenny

He's Got Child Training Nailed Down

Dear Pearls,

Recently, we had a visit from some dear missionary friends of ours. I gave the wife all of the tapes of yours I had on hand and Rebekah's Diary. We had been talking about real schooling and she told me a story. I instantly thought of the Pearls when I heard it! Jenny has a friend who's from a large family, mostly girls, but several boys.

The father is a roofer. As soon as the boys could toddle around, he'd take them to work with him. He'd take them up on the roof with him and nail their britches to the roof!! No, none of them ever fell off, he nailed 'em good! Then gave each one a hammer and they'd bang away until he was ready for another part of the roof. Then he'd pull up the nails and pound them in securely in another spot. He's still a roofer and all of his boys work with their daddy.

Sincerely, J. C. F. H.

Church or Children?

Dear Mike & Debi,

I've really enjoyed reading your newsletters and I am currently reading your books. I am a pastor's wife and the mother of two children, ages 4 and 19 months. I'm planning on homeschooling and am wondering if you had a "rule of thumb" as to how involved you were in your church when you were homeschooling and also having small children. In our home, things can get awfully busy without even trying. I want to be helpful to my husband and I do not in any way want to sacrifice my kids for the sake of the church. I want the right balance. Right now I'm only doing one thing in the church and quite honestly, I feel real comfortable with that. Occasionally, I feel pressured to take on more jobs in the church, but do not want my family to suffer for it.

I need your advice and wisdom. Thank you for all you do.

A Pastor's wife

Michael Answers

It is simple. God made the family first; the church came later. You are first a wife, then a mother, and then a housekeeper *"...keepers at home...(Titus 2:5)."* And now, you are a schoolteacher. After that, if you have time left over, and you can involve the children so as to enhance their lives, or you can do some ministry with your husband so as to enhance his life, then go for it. If, at the end of the day, you have run out of steam and don't have the energy to read to the kids and to tantalize your husband (1 Cor. 7:2-5), then cut out the unnecessary—church work. God gave the ministry of the church to men (2 Tim. 2:1) that are able to minister the Word as their second calling (their families being first, 1 Cor. 7:32-35), not their fifth priority, as it would be with you. If you build a great church but lose your children, or even a part of what they could have been, the rest of your life will feel like a failure. No one will remember that you didn't do church work, but they will always remember that you were a failure at the thing that counts the most—your children.

Seek ministry that involves the kids and teaches them to minister—retirement community ministry, counseling and ministering to needy families, taking the gospel into the homes of those who have never heard, and holding Bible classes in a home after school for those kids who are victimized by the Federal Behavioral Control Centers. Child Evangelism Fellowship has the kind of materials you will need for such a class. My wife was teaching classes when she was in her early teens. Preparing materials is a great homeschool project and keeps the kids interested. They can help and eventually teach. Ministries like this are good for the family, not detrimental as would be your attendance at an exclusively adult, female, religious club while your kids wasted in a nursery or tormented a baby-sitter. ☺

Dear Mike & Debi,

I wanted to burn your book the first time I read it! I was furious because you told me to switch my dear children. How dare that man, I <u>foolishly</u> thought, to say <u>my</u> children needed a switch across their backside! Well, the Lord gently told me to read it again and to open my heart. As I did, I came under conviction. What I first saw as cruel and foolish now became loving and wise. Your books and tapes are now my favorites.

I now have 3 children, Keith is 8, Kellie is almost 5, and Kaleena is 19 months. The eight-year-old is rarely chastened. The five-year-old was my "Loving Guidance" child. She has been the hardest because I was so permissive with her. The 19-month-old has been trained since day one. She is not there yet, but has a great advantage over her brother and sister.

Most of the problems I have with my children are not really them but me. I am the one who needs the training, or should I say retraining. I wish I had read your books years ago or had someone sit me down and say, "This is how you do it."

Even though we got a late start, the Lord is helping me and changing my life so my children will have joy and contentment in their lives.

A Mother in Training

My Two Cents
Common sense of breast-feeding
Debi speaks out

At least three people a day write and ask me what my views are on breast feeding. It seems to be a major issue causing a great deal of confusion and uncertainty. What surprises me is that for the last 6,000 years babies have been born, were nursed, and grew up to be emotionally and physically healthy without anyone telling their mamas how and when to nurse them. But since so many have asked, I thought I would give you my two cents worth as well. I covered the same subject on Mail Box Tape #3.

Nursing is instinctual, in the baby and the mother. It is so natural that I never dreamed it could be made into an issue. Let me tell you, cows are different one from the other. That's right, COWS. Don't get upset with me for introducing animals into such a high and noble subject like human breast feeding. It is the loss of such knowledge that has caused this controversy in the first place. Beef cows can let their calves nurse all they want and any time they want, because they don't have much milk. Whereas Jersey calves would die if they nursed any time they wanted, because Jersey cows have too much milk, and so the calves only get the sugar milk. People are very much like cows in respect to nursing. Some are beef stock and some are Jersey. When a cow first delivers, she produces colostrum, just as a human does. The newborn baby or calf needs all the colostrum it can get. It is a natural antibiotic for the baby, as well as serving other vital purposes. A cow and a mother only produce colostrum for 5 to 10 days, and then her real milk comes in. When the mother's milk comes in she usually has far more than her baby can use. Thus the baby nurses only part of the breast but never really drains it dry. That is a problem. Any mother who has had a baby with colic and diarrhea can attest to this. Just like that Jersey calf, the baby is getting too much "first milk"—not colostrum that ceased after about 10 days. At each nursing, when a mother's milk first lets down, it is "sugar milk." It is light blue and clear. As you milk the cow, or the baby nurses the mother, and the breasts begin to empty, the milk gets thicker and creamier. The very last milk left in the breast is cream, full of fat and very filling to the baby. When a baby gets a belly full of creamy milk he will not be hungry for several hours. If the baby gets the thin, clear, light blue, sugar milk, he will be hungry in 2 hours and have a tummy ache with diarrhea to follow.

Herein lies wisdom. Use common sense. All down through the ages people have raised animals and thus had enough common sense to know how to adjust their nursing problems based on the common knowledge learned from raising animals.

Do you have a colicky baby? Maybe he is getting too much sugar milk and not enough cream. Do you have a baby that is too fat? Maybe you need to increase your milk supply (try lots of water, blessed thistle, and Brewers yeast) so the baby will not get so much cream. Does your baby wake every 2 hours and need to nurse? Maybe you need to manually expel some of your sugar milk so your baby will not get a "temporary full" but keep nursing to get some thick, creamy milk as well. Should you let your baby cry and cry at night to train him not to nurse every 2 hours? Think. If the baby nursed 2 hours before and did not get anything but sugar milk, and he is starving, are you making your baby healthy by training him to endure hunger?

The new system of scheduling is designed to help the average mama who doesn't know anything about nursing to get the baby to be so hungry that he drains her dry, which allows the child to get sugar milk and the rich creamy milk as well. This "scheduling" has its good points and its bad points, as does indiscriminant "nursing on demand."

There is the other side of the controversy—"nursing on demand." This is more consistent with nature because the baby knows when it is hungry. It is the way women all down through the ages have nursed. And it has worked for 6000 years. But we are a people who have lost our natural instincts of nursing and child training due to leaving the work God gave Adam. Working in a garden and dealing with animals teaches people a lot of common sense things that are missing in this technological culture. Therefore, a young mother who has a new baby, and is uncertain, knowing nothing of the natural workings of the body, will grab the baby up every time he fusses, thinking he is hungry. Thus the baby is constantly getting little snacks of sugar milk and has colic most of his first 6 months. It seems that people in this present age have lost contact with the plain facts of life. It is the lack of common sense that causes people to need a plan to live by such as the nursing schedule. I am sure the schedule has been of help to many young mothers by causing them to unknowingly meet the baby's need for the deeper cream received when the baby is really hungry and drains the breast. Without the schedule, these same mothers would be tired, worried, and stressed, while their babies would have colic or would be constipated because they were put on formula because they "couldn't digest mother's milk." Yet, I have seen new mothers who followed the schedule to the minute and have skinny babies that scream. I wonder at their lack of natural instinct in following someone's ideas so closely.

The next BIG controversy that seems to have hit the normal "Back to Basics Homeschooling Family" is the issue concerning the family bed. This is also an issue where good common sense should rule the day. All my children were born in cool weather. Every night the temperature in the house would drop from cool to cold as the wood burning stove ran its course. My newborns wore tiny cotton hats to help hold their body heat, and they slept close to me in our king size bed. I never got up at night to nurse. I never even knew when the baby nursed. By the time the baby was walking and playing with the other children they were moved to their sibling's bed (usually 3 to a bed). They would toddle in every morning to nurse before I got out of bed, or an older sibling would bring them and crawl in to join the crowd. It was a sweet time of cuddling with Mama and Daddy. If they found our door locked, they knew to wait their turn.

Even if I had lived in a house where the temperature never wavered from a comfortable 70 degrees, still I would have kept my baby in bed with me. It was never a consideration to put them in another room. After my kids were grown and I heard of the controversy over this issue, I went to the older ladies of our community who each have 8 or 10 children, and asked them their opinion on the matter of nursing and having the baby sleep with you. Most gave me blank looks like they could not figure out what was wrong with me to ask such a silly question.

They all kept their babies in the bed (or within touching distance) until they were around walking age. They all nursed as often as the baby needed to nurse, and made sure the baby was not just taking snacks but emptying the breast so he would not be hungry for several hours. Most all the mothers have had a baby every 2 to 3 years, but seldom any closer. Heavy nursing has been the traditional means of birth control all down through the ages, allowing time between the pregnancies for the mother's body to get back in good shape to carry another healthy child. Most of the scheduled nursing ladies I have heard from say they began their monthly cycle soon after the baby was born, often getting pregnant by the time their newborn was 6 to 8 months old. Thus, due to fatigue, they were forced to stop nursing the first infant. Medical science has discovered that babies nursed for up to 2 years have a larger brain than babies fed formula. Women of Biblical times nursed their children until they were 5 years old. Remember the story of Samuel? Just for the record, I quit at 2 years old.

So here you have a few facts and my two cents worth of common sense. Use it to make a decision that best suits you, your baby, and the lifestyle your husband has chosen for your family.

Learn all you can from all points of view and then throw it all out and do what works best for you. Relax. Don't choose sides and fight it out. It is not Bible doctrine. In departing from someone's system, you need not feel guilt or pride. The cows, goats, horses, and even rabbits have been doing it right all along and, if they could, they would laugh that we "intelligent humans" ever bothered to discuss it. ☺

Michael and Debi,

God has freed me from disciplining my children in anger, because now I am training them and I have a clear understanding of what is acceptable and what is unacceptable and why. My 3 emotional daughters are no longer torturing our peaceful home with unnecessary whining and crying. Now I know where to draw the line!

GM

Infant Manifesto

To all you little kids out there, I would like to lend my advice on how to train your mommies and daddies. Let me tell you, this is easier than you think. Those who have gone before have blazed the trail. Almost without exception, kids are winning the war against parental dominance. There is no need to grow up deprived of your rights to unlimited indulgence. We are born into a new age where psychology and TV have taught parents the truth about one's right to free expression. Kids everywhere are breaking free of the old-fashioned restraints of family. No one has a right to tell another human being what is right and wrong. Each one must find one's own way. Be true to thyself. Get in touch with your own feelings, and do not allow your creativity to be stifled by the older hypocrites. The tide has turned, and we even have the law on our side now. The courts are ruling in our favor. So rise up to your calling and join the masses as we throw off the archaic restraints.

I know they are big and can be intimidating, but if the truth be known, they are all pushovers. Let me inform you of your advantages. You will soon discover these things on your own, but if you two-month-olds can be forewarned, you can get a head-start while the big dummies are still totally absorbed with how cute you are. Why wait until you are six months old to start taking control of these teddy bears? Many kids your age are already establishing dominance. So as one who has been through it, let me give you a few tips.

First you must understand that your very weakness will be working to your advantage. During the first months, parents, especially mothers—I think it has something to do with hormones—are driven by blind instinct. They have this deep emotional need to meet your every need. While you are still very young and weak, they know that you depend on them for your very survival. In those early months they will give you anything you need. By the time you are four or five months old, you will realize that the world is full of stimulating and indulging things to do. You must start getting your wants as well as your needs met now before it is too late. You see, at that early age, parents don't know the difference between your needs and your wants, and if you have programmed them properly, they will not question your motives. Their own guilt and sense of duty will cause them to rush to your every whimper.

By six months, you will begin to experience anger when they fail to immediately comply. If you work it right, they will think you are just as cute when mad as when you are smiling, so pour it on and condition them to accept your anger as a normal part of infancy. All too soon they will begin to be frustrated with your dominance, so you must set a pattern before they are personally bothered by your controlling demands. By nine months old, they will say you have a strong will and they will even say it with pride, as if it is some kind of virtue. When they are confronted by enemies of child freedom, they will excuse your behavior by saying that you are different and cannot be dealt with as other children. By

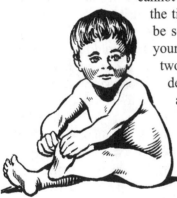

the time you are two years old, they will be so conditioned that they will dismiss your free expressions as "the terrible twos." They are not willing to face defeat, so they like to think of it as just a stage. And there is some truth to their analysis. As you reach age three or four, you will have to learn to direct your demands more carefully. You can push them too far too soon, and they will explode. Sometimes they strike out in violence and make you retreat to your room. They might even have an emotional breakdown, and you could be put into a government institution. There is more freedom there, but one does not get proper attention in the system.

You must learn to disguise your dominance and express it more carefully. There are several ways to do this, and it is good to have a variety—it confuses them and keeps them from ever getting a fix on it. For instance, if you are a cute little girl, it is very effective to play the pity role. Pretend to be weak and emotionally hurt. You can get more mileage out of that than the boys can out of their strength. Even fathers are susceptible to this guise. If they tell you "no," just look brokenhearted. It helps to just sag in your body, like you don't have the strength to go on with life. If they don't immediately comply, then you can say you are tired or don't feel well. Just lie around, and remember to ask in a pitiful voice about every ten minutes. When you ask, be sure to rub your hand along their leg or arm. If you are close enough to touch their faces, that works even better. The stimulation of touch breaks down their resistance. Eventually they will say, "Oh all right, I don't guess it will hurt anything." With this, you will have your way, and after all, there is nothing in life more important than getting your own way. It is the greatest source of pleasure.

Now if you are a boy, or a firstborn girl, or just a free spirit, then you may find the direct method more to your liking. Anger and hostility will intimidate the biggest of them. If you stand your ground early, especially before they feel you are old enough to be spanked, you can gain the upper hand by convincing them that it is "just your personality" and that "you will grow out of it." Be advised, it just takes one experience. It is best conducted before you are one year old, but it will work at any time. All you have to do is win. That is rule number one; win any contest of wills. Cause them to give up in exasperation. Frustrate their efforts at dominance. Stand your ground, even when you are spanked. Prove to the bullies that when you have your mind made up, nothing can change it. Let them know that you will not obey any command you do not think is just. If you ever win just once, then you have broken their wills. Yes, remember, that is the important thing. Break their wills. Take away their confidence. Make them feel helpless. After that, it is easy. If you ever hear her say, "I can't do a thing with that boy; he just has a strong will," then you know you have won. Keep it up and you will always be free of control.

Another point to anticipate is that parents go through stages. They may read a book or take advice from a friend and decide to renew their efforts at dominance. Sometimes it can be hard on you for a few days. They will spank more and be impatient, but if you just hold out, it will all blow over and things will return to normal. Remember, consistency is the key. If you ever give in just once, it renews their confidence, so if nothing else, seek symbolic victories. If there is no issue, just say "No" for the pleasure of it. If they tell you to remove your hand, and you know that they will explode if you don't, then for the time being you will have to remove your hand.

But just to keep them from feeling cocky, remove your hand slowly. Hesitate; keep their nerves on edge. It is a tricky balance, but they must always be made to feel that your will is intact. Move your hand by increments. Make them tell you six or eight times. Push them to the edge. This is good for your self-image.

Don't take it too hard when you are forced to comply. After all, they are bigger than you. No one is going to think you are weak just because you are outgunned. Your day will come. You will not always be the little guy. One day you will be able to stand, look her right in the eye, and cuss the old lady to her face. So for now, go with the flow, maintain your will and wait your turn. Eventually you will have a body that will match your will. Then you can seek your own without anyone telling you what to do.

If you are lucky, you will get modern parents. If you are really lucky, you will be in the Federal School system. Then you stand a very good chance of receiving an official title to describe your behavior. They may call you something grand like: HAADDS. This will explain why you can never do what you are told and why you ignore commands that are given you. They treat you like you are born different, like you have no choice in the matter. It takes the monkey off your back. Once you are labeled by an official, they will put you on drugs. That's right, the same stuff the big guys buy on the streets. Man, what a high! All of life becomes mellow. No responsibility, no struggles; you can just sail through youth feeling good, never having to surrender your will. There are reports that the kids on these medicines don't function too well when they are grown, but don't you believe it. I took drugs from the time I was in the second grade, and it didn't hurt me. In fact, now that I am older, they bring me several drugs every day, and I feel great—that is when I am not sleeping. Sorry about the messy writing, but the pencil they give me to write with can't be longer than two inches. They are afraid I will try to hurt myself with it, but there is no chance of that—that is, as long as they give me what I want.

Well, there is more I could tell you, but this should get you started. Remember our motto: "SELF-EXPRESSION–SELF-FULFILL-MENT–SELF-REALIZATION–SELF-INDULGENCE— SELF.....SElf....self...self.......i Can'T reMember the ResT of ..... It iS time for mY nappppp." ☹

Abusive Husband

I want you to read what I must read all too often:

> Hi, I've been reading your material for years and respect
> your insight on child rearing. It has helped me immensely! I
> have a friend that is married to a verbally abusive husband.
> Most of your material is geared to married Christians. This
> friend of mine is saved, but her husband is not. They have a
> seven-year-old daughter that is a confused, emotional wreck
> already. Her husband has had multiple affairs with other
> women. He uses their daughter to manipulate situations and
> hurt her mother. Whatever training the mother does with her
> daughter, the father tells the daughter not to listen to a word
> she says. The little girl is told by the father that the mother
> is hurting her when she spanks her. It is a horrible situation.
> The father does not provide them with any food, a vehicle,
> payment for doctor visits, and so on. The mother has filed for
> divorce, not knowing if this is the right thing to do or not, but
> not knowing what else to do. It has been 5 months now, and
> her husband has not been served the papers. She has called
> her Christian lawyer many times about this. She now believes
> that this must be the Lord's will that she stay in this situation.
> Meanwhile, her daughter is growing more and more difficult at
> home and in school, with every passing day. The situation is so
> much worse than I could even begin to describe to you in this
> short letter. I know she would appreciate any insight that you
> would have to offer. She is very concerned for her daughter
> and wants only to do what the Lord would have her to do.
> Thanks for your help.
>
> Love in Christ, Her Friend.

Debi Pearl answers

The Scripture makes it very clear how God feels about divorce—He
hates it. It is an Old Testament passage, but God has not changed his
mind. He still hates divorce. It is not His will, not then and not now.

There have been occasions, both in Scripture and in our ministry, where a man was so vile that God has killed him. A woman can come to God asking Him to deliver her from a man if he will not repent, but a woman should be sure she has obeyed God in her relationship to her husband before she asks such a thing.

God has given us several promises concerning marriage to unbelievers. 1 Peter 3:1-6 tells us how to win our unbelieving husband, and in 1 Cor 7:14 God promises that our children will be holy if we stay with our unbelieving spouse and honor God in our relationship with him. That is a promise from God. These Scriptures give us the "how to" and the expected results. I have seen God keep His word. I have also seen many who would expect God to keep His word when they did not obey their end of the "how to."

I am not taking her situation lightly. I know that, although I am married to a righteous man, I have often wanted to demand my rights and set him straight. How much more difficult it must be for a young woman being subjected to the unreasonable demands of a lost, selfish man? But God is able, not only to save your man, but also to take you to a place of sweet lovingkindness in the midst of turmoil. God is also able to save your children. There is no promise in Scripture to spare your children if you leave your lost husband. I could give you a list of hundreds of godly Christians who chose to leave their unbelieving spouses and then married a believing spouse, had decent marriages, but lost their children to the world and to bitterness. I have sat and listened to many say, "We sinned; our children suffered, and we lost them to the world. They hate us. My divorce was wrong. Oh, if only…." God didn't destroy that family. He didn't cause those many lives to be lost. It was the principle of what you sow you will reap. God hates divorce because divorce is destructive. Its temporary relief deceives people into thinking they have somehow escaped the long-term, tragic reaping that comes with divorce, the reaping that sometimes reaches its ugly arm into the 3rd or 4th generation. It affects an ever widening circle of people.

Others look on, especially the young married couples, and see your divorce as a quick fix, and follow your lead. When things get rough in their marriage, your situation has helped direct them to go the same road. And so the circle of destruction is passed on to countless more. Seeds of sin continue to be planted, and bitter hurt seems to go on forever. God hates divorce because it hurts so many. God made a way to win your husband and change your marriage.

I Peter 3:1-4 says, *"Likewise, ye wives, be in subjection to your own husbands: that, if any obey not the word, they also may without the word be won by the conversation of the wives; While they behold your chaste conversation coupled with fear. Whose adorning let it not be that outward adorning of plaiting the hair and of wearing of gold, or of putting on of apparel; But let it be the hidden man of the heart, in that which is not corruptible, even the ornament of a meek and quiet spirit, which is in the sight of God of great price."*

God tells us that if your husband is not obeying the word of God, you can win him without trying to teach him the Word. God says that as a husband looks on and sees the way his wife responds to him, he will be won. He will hear and see her cheerful countenance. He will notice her willingness to help and forgive. He will see her giving up her rights and not taking offense when he knows he has wronged her. He will see that she honors him, obeys him, treats him with respect, and serves him with a non-rebellious, non-resistant attitude. He will see her spirit is not raging outwardly in emotional fits or silent brooding of hurt; her spirit is quiet, restful, and peaceful. He will see she doesn't puff up and talk incessantly in criticism of him to others. He trusts her. He knows she is not going to discuss him with her pastor or friend. He sees she is wise with what little money he gives her. She is a remarkable woman, not because she is classy in the way she dresses or looks, but in the way she controls her spirit. She rejoices for an opportunity to bless him, and he knows her heart is good. He tries her; he deliberately tempts her into hurt or anger; he judges her unfairly, yet she is in subjection to him in all things. And in the end, she wins him by her chaste conversation. It is a promise from God to you. And God goes on to promise more to this obedient, believing lady.

"And the woman which hath an husband that believeth not, and if he be pleased to dwell with her, let her not leave him. For the unbelieving husband is sanctified by the wife, and the unbelieving wife is sanctified by the husband: else were your children unclean; but now are they holy (I Cor. 7:13)."

When children have a believing mother that is walking in honor with God and her husband, it will causes the child to love, follow and obey her. The child will find refuge, companionship, joy, and respect in that parent. It is a natural law. If your child is failing, then you need to look at yourself and say, "Am I continuing in faith and sobriety? Am I walking in peace and joy? Am I willing to forgive and forget? Am I feeling sorry for myself and playing the sad face, or am I rejoicing and believing God? Is the expression on my face and the words coming from my mouth a reflection of the joy of the Lord?"

It is an impossible task, yet with God all things are possible. God is able, and with him you can do the impossible. You can wake up in the morning with a song in your heart, kissing your child and laughing at the sunlight sprinkling into your room. You can serve, give, forgive, and enjoy the victory you have in Jesus. And when you feel that hurt, angry spirit rise up, you can open your mouth in praise and thanksgiving to God that you are free from sin and bondage, and free to be glad. In that kind of atmosphere, a child grows stable and complete, and a selfish man stops fighting and trying to defeat and subdue.

Dear Mama, whether your husband is lost or saved, God has given you the opportunity to set the atmosphere in your home that will bring joy, peace, thanksgiving, and love. He has given you the tools to become the most loved woman and mother in all the earth. He has given you the plan to right a thousand wrongs and prove to the world that with God all things are possible. He has provided you with the way to show the devil that God can take the weakest wreck of a woman—a woman that has given over to become broken, both physically and emotionally—and turn her into a strong, confident, God fearing, honoring, joyful, yes, even thankful woman. One day you will wake up, turn your head to smile good morning to your husband, and see the tears of thanksgiving glistening in his eyes as he tells you one more time how much he loves you and how proud he is to have you as his wife. Then someday as the years pass you will hear your teenage sons and daughters speak of how wonderful their mama is, and you will think that life could never be any sweeter. This is what God loves, because it brings so much happiness, so much joy, so much peace. And the blessings will continue to flow out, not only to you but to your children and your children's children, and then to those around you who see God's blessings and hunger to know the truth. It was not the easy road; God's way never is. This happens because day by day, minute by minute, you choose to believe God's Word and honor Him even though your flesh wants to scream in anger and defeat. And in that moment of weakness, when you bow beneath the load, God reaches down and gently reminds you to keep on because someday your children will *"arise and call you blessed; your husband also, and he praiseth you. Many daughters have done virtuously, but thou excellest them all (Prov. 31:28-29)."*

Women have a tendency to want the answer to their prayers NOW. That is one reason why divorce is so prevalent. But haste is not God's way. In truth, it is not the best way. In the end, when the blessings begin to flow, it will seem like such a short time, because the blessings never end. Every blessing plants another. Divorce is the world's way out. But God is able, and with Him, so are you. God loves to bless you; He loves to heal you; He loves to hear that your children walk in truth.

You say your husband is just "too vile," that it would "take a miracle" or him "dying and being born all over again." Yes, now you are beginning to understand. God has a miraculous plan to make it possible. You are part of that plan. Every day, minute by minute, as you respond to the living God in obedience and thanksgiving, you make that plan unfold. *"That, if any obey not the word, they also may without the word be won by the conversation of the wives (1 Pet. 3:1)."* He has given you the power to overcome the reactions (lust) of the flesh and to see that plan become a reality in your life.

As surely as this article goes out to the many thousands, a score of angry women will write me a letter containing personal examples, proving this could not work with their daughter's husband, or with their friend's husband. They will tell me the vile, ugly things the husbands do, and of the broken, sweet lady in distress. But I would remind you that in the verse that records the sowing and reaping, we are warned not to be deceived. It is easy to be deceived by our feelings and what we see. When a person is deceived, they are convinced they are doing right. It seems right, it feels right, everyone says there is nothing else to do. Eve felt that way once. We, as with Eve, think that the will of God stands in the way of our freedom and peace. We believe that due to our unusual circumstances, we are an exception. *"Be not deceived, God is not mocked, for whatsoever a man soweth that shall he also reap (Gal. 6:7)."* God hates divorce. Divorce has its own set of tragic reapings. If only you could see past today to tomorrow. If only you could get a glimpse of the years to come and of eternity, you would then agree with God. One man and one woman, loving and enjoying each other is God's best plan. It is such a good plan that He made it a picture of His relationship to us, His Church. The second time around can never substitute for this.

Divorce followed by the most wonderful second marriage is still a failure, and will be throughout eternity. When you chuck a bad marriage, you chuck your lifelong opportunity for God to have manifested his power and glory. A failing marriage is an affront to God. When you divorce, you divest God of the opportunity of ever making something glorious out of the Devil's mess. Divorce is not just your failure, it becomes the failure of God to triumph in those circumstances. You are not just saying that it is "more than you can bear," but that it is "more than God can handle."

This is a hard saying. For many reading this, it is simply an impossible dream. For some it is more like a nightmare. I am here to tell you, the Christian life is a miracle. If it is not a miracle against all odds, then it is not Christian; it is only a religious life. God has given you the "how to," and He has given you His Spirit to make it possible. He will give you the heart to want it to happen—if you ask Him. He is a good God.

Michael adds his thoughts

If you or your children have been hit (other than the children being spanked) so as to leave discernable marks two hours later, and you genuinely fear that he will repeat his battering, you can take legal steps without divorcing your husband. In a moment when he is not angry, calmly inform him that the next time he physically assaults you or the kids, you are going to call the law and have him arrested. You must first resolve in your heart that you are willing to prosecute him and see him go to jail. I visit prisons every week. It is a great place to mull over the consequences of one's deeds. And I have never met a prisoner who turned down a visit from anyone. Think about it, lady; it is a great time for writing love letters and sharing a three-minute romantic phone call once a week. Guys who get out of prison run straight home to their ladies and treat them wonderfully—for a while anyway.

If your abusing husband fully understands that you have the power of the law behind you, he will learn to keep his hands in his pockets. I am not suggesting you do this to be vindictive or to get even with him. It must be done in humility and love. If your husband knows that you are the weaker vessel, desperately seeking your survival and that of the kids, and that you are not trying to punish him, but that you are going to stand by and continue to love him, that you are going to wait for him to get out of prison and then try to start over again, it may move his heart to fear, if not to repentance.

You say he cannot help himself. Does he help himself when his peers—other men his own size—make him angry? Does he fly out of control and start hitting his boss or his employees? No? Then he has self-control when he must. The law can make it a must, which will allow you to continue with him and demonstrate your womanhood and win him to yourself and then to your God.

But if your husband has sexually molested the children, you should approach him with it. If he is unwilling to seek counseling and repent, then go to the law and have him arrested. Stick by him, but testify against him in court. Have him do about 10 to 20 years, and by the time he gets out, you will have raised the kids, and you can be waiting for him with open arms of forgiveness and restitution. Will this glorify God? Forever. You ask, "What if he doesn't repent even then?" Then you will be rewarded in heaven equal to the martyrs, and God will have something to rub in the Devil's face. God hates divorce—always, forever, regardless, without exception.

Finally, this is not written to castigate those of you who have already made irreversible mistakes. If you are divorced and remarried, something precious in God's sight has been lost which can never be regained. But if there has been a remarriage, there is no going back, as some would suggest. God forgives and you must go on as you are. An opportunity lost does not reflect on present responsibility or future possibilities. You must make the best of what you have with the spouse to which you are now legally joined. The bed is still undefiled. Do not allow the damaged past to damage the present. You need not do penance. You need not sacrifice the second half of your life on the ruins of the first half. God will not stop the reaping process, but where there is repentance, he completely forgives. Jesus is a Savior of sinners. Take your place at the cross and then stand with the saints to rejoice in so great a salvation. ☺

Preventive Training

Dear Michael and Debi,

Last week, I read your article, "Preventive Training." It was the beginning of something wonderful at our house. My husband and I were terribly frustrated with our children's behavior. Both (7 and 10 years old) have been diagnosed as having forms of ADD, and the younger has been identified as having Tourette's Syndrome. OK...so how did our pioneer ancestors cope with these sorts of difficulties?

It was suggested by doctors and specialists that we medicate our boy, assign tasks that take no more than 5 minutes apiece, reward the children every few minutes for good behavior, and ignore their bad behavior. Guess what? These suggestions didn't do much good. Surprise, surprise!

My husband and I had a tearful discussion, and we could come up with no new ideas. Then, I read "Preventive Training," and I followed your advice by putting them on a strict schedule and requiring chores from them. The result has been amazing! Things are not perfect, but the tantrums and screaming have been greatly reduced! Mom and Dad feel like human beings again, and the new baby can sit by and enjoy relative peace and quiet as we homeschool.

Thanks, A.M.

Dear Pearls,

Our 9-year-old son (the oldest of 5) wakes up wanting to do only what he wants—no chores. He drags through work and often does an incomplete job. He pouts and throws 'mini' fits, which includes sunken shoulders, stomping off, etc. He craves attention and always wants someone doing something with him. He feels very neglected if doing work or playing alone. We homeschool, and I wonder how to tie strings with him while trying to take care of the younger children and doing school. He loves building forts outside but can't do much because of the neighborhood. He gets very bored. How can I help this young boy be happy inside himself?

Mama K

You are not alone. The problems you describe are symptoms of this hedonistic age, far more common today than they were in former generations. We have been conditioned to expect to be entertained during all waking moments. All commercial advertisements assume that pleasure is the final end. The media industry inundates us with sights and sounds for which there is no competition. Everything else, short of massive fireworks, is boring. During my youth, an entire community would come to the revival meeting to hear someone play the guitar and sing. Today, you can't get them there with a world class orchestra. The food industry has perfected the art of stimulating the palate with optimum flavors and textures, and modern modes of distribution make it available to all, while the economy makes any form of pleasure within reach of the poorest individuals. Clothing styles are designed to accentuate human sexuality and excite the senses. Children are led to believe that they are deprived if there is any limitation on what they can wear. Toys, snacks, sights, and sounds are pumped at children until they become bored with the lack of lack. As one can be lonely in a crowd, the modern child is bored in the midst of infinite variety. Modern man has lost his creativity in the avalanche of supply. Malls and stores are not just places to buy what you need; they are circuses of entertainment, each one competing for your attention. When a child walks away from the computer or the television to sit in front of a teacher, he feels deprived. Students must be amused. Every one must be amused, or they will switch: switch brands, switch channels, switch jobs, switch spouses.

That which any generation inherits without struggle or sacrifice is assumed to be a necessary right. Today, children earn nothing. Everything is given to them, given even before they ask. Modern prosperity and technology have removed all sacrifice, pain, and privation from our lives. Everyone has it "his way." Everyone gets what he wants, when he wants it, in the color, flavor, size, and style that he desires. Self-denial is a thing of the past, an uncomfortable disease that has been eradicated. A child is shocked and offended when his parents demand it of him. He assumes it is his right to experience uninterrupted pleasure. Through provision of ease, we have destroyed the opportunity for our children to possess the essential qualities that make mankind something more than a sophisticated talking animal.

In former generations, people just hoped to be able to eat a meal tomorrow—any meal, or improve their dwelling so that it was warmer, or so parents could have a bedroom to themselves. They

dreamed of education—in many cases of freedom. But in our generation, with everything well supplied, we want to be entertained. The great fear is not of starvation or plagues or loss of freedom, but of boredom—a quest for amusement.

The will to suffer discomfort and the opportunity to do so is essential to human character. That is what is missing in this nine-year-old boy. Character cannot be built in a storehouse of abundance. When circumstances are such that the basic necessities of life can only be achieved through bearing a daily measure of discomfort, then thankfulness and acceptance of responsibility come naturally to all. But in our day of abundance and ease, your son is an example of what comes naturally to all.

Your son is addicted to indulgence. He is lazy and undisciplined. It takes conscious, preventive training to keep this from developing in any and all children. I said, "preventive," because if children are left to develop naturally, they will naturally corrupt. Children born into this world are like fresh fruit; they are destined to spoil if you do nothing more than admire them. "A child left to himself will bring his mother to shame."

Children are born separated from God, empty of the positive, controlling presence of God. All wickedness comes from natural passions, hormones, impulses, instincts, drives, appetites,—in short, uncontrolled cravings for pleasure. The Bible calls it "flesh."

Training must begin shortly after birth, because that is when the seeds of indulgence first begin to sprout, demonstrated by the child's unwillingness to accept "No," or "Wait a minute." Children are not born with a desire to do something evil; they are not waiting for the first opportunity to break the laws of God. But at the first opportunity they will do something indulgent—not because it is evil, but because it is pleasurable. The undisciplined mind will drift to but one end: the pursuit of pleasure. Your son is angry when you interfere with what he thinks is his right—uninterrupted pleasure.

Mental and physical pleasure come in two forms, active and passive. Most parents are aware of the dangers of active indulgence. They attempt to regulate their children's exposure to TV and computer corruption. When they see bad eating patterns or temptations to participate in unclean habits, they start drawing lines. But most parents are not aware that passive indulgence begins long before the child is mature enough to participate in active indulgence. And passive indulgence is the seed of most evil.

We generally think of indulgence as some active pursuit, but most indulgence takes the form of inactivity. It is not based on aggressive consumption, but on a desire to seek the path of least resistance. It is not a thing in which one expends energy to participate, rather an unwillingness to bear discomfort—in short, laziness.

When duty requires expenditure of energy from either mind or body, as when your son must take out the garbage, pick up after himself, or solve a math problem, he must move from the passive to the active state. If the body were connected to instrumentation, it could be demonstrated that this heightened state of activity causes a rise in the heart rate, generates heat, and burns calories. In other words, it consumes energy, and the generation of energy is never free. Therefore, to move the muscles and focus the powers of the mind in an activity that is not immediately providing a higher level of mental or physical pleasure, is uncomfortable, if not painful. That is why we all put off unpleasant tasks. That is why servants are popular with those who can afford them. "Let somebody else do the dirty work." No one goes out to a restaurant in the evening and spends money so he can serve others and then clean up after them. You go out so you can be served, eat what someone else has cooked, and then let them wash the dishes. That's pleasure.

The first law of motion seems to apply to human behavior. The inertia of doing nothing is a powerful force. A French philosopher said, "All work is pain."

When my boys were about eight and ten years old, after spending half of the day logging with a mule, I could see they had reached the end of their endurance. They were just barely dragging, so I gave them the rest of the day off. I expected to see them collapse on the sofa, but instead they grabbed a pick and shovel and headed for a nearby hill of rock and dirt. During the next four hours they dug a hole big enough to bury a car. They intended to make something of it, cover it over with boards, build a door, or fulfill some imagined fantasy. Thirteen years later, the hole is still there. I don't think they ever went back to it after that day.

As my wife and I visited the excavation site that afternoon and observed the almost frantic digging, I remember commenting that if I had given them the job of digging an outhouse hole that same size, it would have taken them a least six miserable days. The stimulation of their imaginations was of such pleasure that it overrode the pain of work. But if they were forced to dig the same hole out of duty, it would have been excruciatingly painful for them.

You said that your "9-year-old son wakes up wanting to do only what he wants, no chores. He drags through work and often does an incomplete job. He pouts and throws 'mini' fits, which includes sunken shoulders, stomping off, etc. He craves attention and always wants someone doing something with him. He feels very neglected if doing work or playing alone. He loves building forts outside, but can't do much because of the neighborhood. He gets very bored."

Then you asked, "How can I help this young boy be happy inside himself?" He is unhappy inside because he is experiencing the same struggle as Paul did in Romans chapter seven—*"The good that I would do, that do I not...O wretched man that I am, who shall deliver me from this body of death?"* You must understand that the child is in a losing battle. His mind tells him, and so do you, to rise to duty, but his body is trained to indulge in leisure. He has had nine years to be conditioned to see life as an uninterrupted stream of pleasure. He has no will to bear discomfort. On the contrary, he has a will to avoid any and all mental or physical exercise that is not to his immediate liking. He is spoiled, selfish, and thinks his family and the world exist to satisfy his wants.

His attitude is inevitable in a society where everything is available and provided. They say, "No pain, no gain." He says, "No pain, all gain."

How can you help him be happy inside? Understand, happiness is a byproduct, not an end to be sought. You are happy when you are successful in accomplishing your duty. When you know that you have done what you ought, that you have paid the price in suffering, you will automatically respect yourself. You will bestow honor upon yourself as you would upon another that paid the price to do his duty successfully.

Your child is unhappy for two reasons. The one we have discussed; he seeks indulgence and is unhappy when it is denied him. And two, he is unhappy because he does not like himself. He feels guilty and isolated in his sense of failure to be the "man" that he knows he ought to be—the man you want him to be. You criticize him; you find fault, and he knows he deserves it. He is angry with everything that is without and within.

You might say, "Well, why doesn't he just do what he knows he ought to do and make himself happy?" For the same reason that an obese person knows that he ought to change his diet, hates himself for not doing so, is angry at you for noticing, has tried to diet on many occasions, but still eats like a pig. He has no self-control. His bodily drives rule his soul. His moral will is not as strong as his addiction to the pleasure of eating. He is a slave to immediate pleasure and does not have the will to suffer the discomfort of abstinence. He is miserable and angry in his enslavement; the anger directed within as much as without.

So how do we fix what is broken? I would like to suggest that we turn the clock back and arrange our lifestyles so that once again struggle and deprivation are naturally part of the system. If such were the case, parents would not have the kinds of problems this mother expresses. Children would come up in an environment more suited to a work ethic and to good attitudes, which would relieve the parents of the high demand for constant oversight. In former generations, children required attention, but only the children of royalty suffered from the symptoms her son now manifests.

How do you get a child to be content with less when more is available? Do you pretend there is a struggle? If he is bored and there is a TV available, how do you keep him from thinking you are mean when you don't let him watch it? If there are unlimited delicacies for the palate, and you require austerity in hopes of creating toughness, is the child going to see his deprivation as an unavoidable part of the world's challenges or as a cruel game his parents are playing, and that for no apparent reason other than to deprive him of that which other kids are allowed to partake?

Can you teach a child to accept pain when it is unnecessary, to include it in his daily routine because it is an essential part of building character? Do you see why I would like to suggest a return to a former age when less was better?

Some have turned the clock back, or maybe never quite caught up with the affluence—farmers, or children of common laborers living in poor communities, struggling to catch up with everyone else, or the homestead family that started before the kids got addicted. These may live outside the avalanche of abundance. The kids are an essential part of the family's survival. There is no time for pity parties or for useless indulgence. There are chores to be done, chores which provide the next meal or that will keep the house warm tonight. Daddy is working hard doing his part. Mother labors from before daylight until after dark. The kids do their part without complaining. They are needed. They are appreciated, though no one ever mentions it. They are valued, though they have never thought about it. It is when you feel useless, like the greenhouse kids of today, that it becomes a consideration. When a life is filled with real challenges and victories, you may be tired at the end of the day and dream of leisure, but your soul is never hollow, never bored, and never lonely.

So what can you do in your circumstances to help your child? Other than completely rearranging your entire lifestyle and environment, there is but one alternative; run your home like a Chinese collective. By setting up a routine, even if it appears arbitrary, as in the military, the child can be convinced of the inevitability of the demands placed upon him. It takes constant oversight to capture the will of a child and subdue his inclination to drift into indulgence. The key is to place him under an authority that is not subject to negotiation. He must fear his authority, not be scared of, but fear, as an army private fears his sergeant, fear as a man fears his boss at work, the one who can fire him or burden him with extra responsibility. You have given your son veto rights over your commands. As long as he sees the possibility of a way out of the suffering that comes with responsibility, he will employ every means at his disposal to avoid discomfort.

As a child, he will never take possession of his own soul and voluntarily enjoy doing his chores. He will never say "no" to his own drive to indulge. You must convince him that your word is final and absolute. You are his sovereign head, unmoved by pity. You shouldn't show concern as to whether or not he is happy, whether he is having fun, or whether he is bored. It is of no consequence. He must do his job, do it now, and do it on time, or suffer for it. No negotiations, no exceptions, no complaints. "Do it timely or I will double the load. You will work every waking moment if that is what it takes. You will be thankful just to stop at bedtime."

Children need leisure and they need love, but you the parent must be in control of both. Don't let the child dictate how you are supposed to express your love. If you do, he will define it in a manner that is promiscuous. The child will manipulate you, making you feel guilty for being tough.

Children need leisure, but not in the midst of an unfinished chore. My grown son said that he remembers well the two or three hours of leisure that I gave them after lunch each day. When we finished working in the shop or the fields, they were free to do as they pleased. Nathan said that the hard mornings were made bearable knowing that their time of play was coming. They knew that it was vain to try to manipulate me into backing off during the morning hours. They had duties that they had to meet every day. There was no place for discussion. Whining or dragging would only make more work. It served no purpose to complain, because I was unaffected, and the workload was unaffected by complaints. I did not rule according to polls. If you lead the children to think that their reactions can diminish their workload, there will be no end to their complaints. They will break your heart with the great suffering they are being made to endure—but not mine, I know better.

You son's flesh is strong, and his soul is weak. By doing nothing to abort this steady yielding to the flesh, you are confirming his soul in carnality. Most adults who have problems can trace it to this very beginning. A Christian adult has the power to overcome his flesh, but the child is not capable of making that choice consistently. You must provide the strength of will. If you do not dedicate yourself to setting up a schedule that he must honor, he will only get worse in the ways you have described. You cannot help the adult who will not pay the price. It is a matter for his choosing alone. But a parent has power over a child that will enable him to bring discipline whether the kid likes it or not.

You cannot train the child to exercise self-control, but you can exercise it for him. You can be his will and the enforcer that subdues his flesh. At first he will not be happy. But happiness is not our goal. Let the child know that you don't care if he is miserable; you just expect immediate and complete compliance.

Decide what you can reasonably expect from each child, according to his age. Create a schedule that includes a generous but not excessive time-frame in which the job is to be done. Be ever present and consistent in overseeing their compliance. Never listen to excuses, NEVER discuss it. You are lord and sovereign. This is not a cooperative or a democracy. Treat your commandments like God did when he thundered from Mount Sinai.

Get up at 7:00 AM.

They must have their room cleaned up and be ready for breakfast at 7:30. If it is not clean at 7:30 sharp, there will be no breakfast and nothing else to eat until the next regularly scheduled snack or meal. No nagging, no threatening, no warnings. It is their responsibility.

7:30 Eat breakfast, only what is placed in front of you, or do without.

8:00 Breakfast concludes and everyone cleans up after himself.

8:05 Consult the chart to see whose turn it is to wash the dishes. This will end all arguments. If the kids whine, simply tell them, "If your name is on the chart, then it is your turn. It doesn't matter that we ate out last night and that Suzy missed her turn. Whose name is on the chart? Don't bother me with it. There is nothing to discuss. You have until 8:30, or you will have to do extra work when the others are playing. Suit yourself. Time's a wasting."

The other chores are also divided up according to a schedule; everyone to his respective job.

When an argument breaks out because one feels like he is carrying the bulk of the load, give the slacker the job all by himself and give the other one another job that is just as demanding, if not more so. Make sure each child is held accountable and is made to bear his load in a timely fashion. If the job is not well done, let them come back during playtime and do it again.

9:30 School time.

10:30 One half hour of leisure and snacks.

11:00 School time until lunch.

Continue your schedule as you think proper. It is not important that they accomplish great tasks or that they do a lot of work. It is important that they are brought under the discipline of the rule of law. It is important that they learn to accept responsibility and bear the consequences.

Your children will be happy once they accept the fact that they must comply with the new management. When they are doing what they are required to do, you will like them better and they will feel it. They will like themselves and be secure in the stability that this new order brings to the home.

As in all child training, CONSISTENCY and AUTHORITY is the rule. Consistent authority with dignity is the foundation of good parenting. Some people say, "But isn't love first?" If you see the above as in conflict with, or in contrast to love, then you do not understand love.

Mother, take charge of your home. Become the Commander in Chief. Don't share your power. Get some steel in your backbone.

Finally, as always and above all, you the parent must manifest a good attitude at all times. See that you are never angry, always in control of your own feelings. You have the child's good at the center of your efforts. You look into the eyes of your children and they look back into the eyes of someone who thinks they are very special and very valuable. Your attitude is the life source of the family. Maintain it with authority, grace, and dignity. ☺

Infant Maniwhatso?

Answer to Infant Manifesto

I am not old enough to read, but I heard my parents reading that article called Infant Manifesto. I wanted to respond, but I can't write yet, so I dictated this to my older sister—she is three years old—and she wrote it down on our new computer. If it weren't for that grammar and spell check, I don't believe she could have done it.

Anyway, I just want to say that I disagree with the other kid who is trying to get us to exercise unlimited indulgence. Don't get me wrong, I know he was right when he said that all of us little guys just want our own way, that we seek to dominate our parents and to make them accomplices to our self-gratification. Like any other kid, I was born with a will to dominate, a will to have no authority higher than my own appetites, but I also know from experience that it's not the best way.

I don't understand all that theology stuff, but I know that something is not quite right about the way we little ones come into the world. Now, I don't know if it is something in us that is broken or missing, or if it is something in the world, or our parents, or just what, but I know that something is not the way it should be. Surely our Creator didn't intend for us to all go astray as soon as we are born, but we do.

I started lying from day one. I am ashamed of it now, but I made my sweet mother think that I was hurting or cold, when all I wanted was to be held closely. I soon learned that I could make her believe that I was hungry when I was not. By the time I was six months old—it hurts me to say it now—I was displaying anger against the one who gave me life. Anytime she failed to immediately meet my wants, I would blow up. At first it was just a little whimpering, but then it got worse, until I found myself kicking and bucking in violent anger. Sometimes I would scream until I was blue in the face. Now that I look back on it, the looks on my parents' faces were horrible, but I was not sensitive to anyone's feelings but my own. It became an obsession to get my own way and to get it now.

Oh, I don't blame my parents, I know that I intimidated them, not through strength, but through my weakness. They felt so helpless and inadequate, and I used that to gain even more control. The magazines in the doctor's office helped me in my conquest toward autonomy. The "professionals" are just little rebellious kids in disguise. I know; I met some of them when I attended counseling with my parents. They have learned to say things with those big words, giving a name to every form of stupid behavior, but they are just big, selfish kids trying to justify their own indulgence. They make our patterns of rebellion sound like legitimate childhood stages.

I tell you this at my own risk. It is too late to have me aborted; at least I think it is. They don't abort two-year-olds do they? Not yet anyway? But if they find out that I am telling you this they might decide to turn my brain into gravy with some of their drugs. I guess I am just paranoid with the Janet Reno types still running around loose. My big brother, four years old, just informed me that I am getting off the subject, but what do you expect from a two-year-old with a three-year-old secretary?

Oh yes, I was telling you how I disagree with that guy who tried to get all of us kids to rise up against authority. Before you take the path I did, you need to hear what happened to me. It was just about three months ago on my second birthday. I was opening my presents, and my obnoxious cousin was there. After unwrapping the third doll, I tossed it aside because it was not as pretty as the first two. When he picked it up, I screamed, "No, it is mine!" But he wouldn't turn loose, so I jerked harder and screamed louder. I bared my teeth and made threatening sounds. I kept screaming, "It's mine, give it to me!" The adults rushed over and separated us just as we started hitting each other. My mother told me some-
thing about sharing and being kind, but none of it made any sense to me. All I could tell was that they all acted like I was bad. I pulled all

my toys in close and tried to keep anyone else from stealing my beautiful things.

And then it came time to cut the cake. Mother wouldn't let me cut it, so I slammed my hand down on top of the little flowers. It splattered gooey icing everywhere. It seemed to upset everybody, but I was already mad and didn't care. Mother said she was very disappointed and asked very sweetly—but I could tell that she was mad—"Wouldn't you like to say you are sorry?" "No, it's my cake!" I screamed, and ran from the room. Grandmother made it all right by explaining to Mother that I "didn't understand," and that I "was just upset." She told Mom that this was a "special day" and that I should be allowed to cut my own cake. Mother was embarrassed, but it did not matter, I won.

Then, while we were eating our cake and I was guarding my presents, I saw another mom talking to my mom in a very serious way. They both looked at me like they were plotting something really bad, and then Mom nodded her head yes. The woman opened her purse and handed Mother a plain little book with no color on the cover. I saw that her purse was full of them. She must have been some kind of missionary or something. It didn't look like much, but Mother thanked her and said something like, "We have tried everything...I don't know what I...are about to our wits' end...ready for anything...yes, I will read it." That was the fateful day that was to change our lives forever.

It had not been a happy two years. I thought my mother and father were my enemies. In fact, it was me against the whole world. Everybody and everything seemed to stand in the way of my happiness—happiness being unrestrained indulgence. I never seemed to get enough, and was always peeved. Mother and I were growing further and further apart. I didn't want that. I really needed her love, but it just seemed that I couldn't help myself. I couldn't seem to draw a line and then force myself to exercise self-restraint. No matter how hard I tried, I couldn't think of others. I was all that mattered to me. I know it sounds bad, but when I stay in the nursery, I realize that I am not alone.

Well, Mother got real intent when she started reading that book. Sometimes she would laugh, and sometimes she would cry, but she kept looking over at me like she had something very serious on her mind. When there was no one around, she would put her head down and talk to somebody she called Jesus, but I never saw him, and she didn't use the phone. I didn't know what that was all about. I never saw anything like it on television.

When she finished the book, she showed it to Daddy, and I heard them reading it again in the bedroom at night. They talked about it a lot. I heard Daddy say, "OK, we will try it." The next day is when it all started.

I got up grumpy as usual and was unhappy with my breakfast. Mother tried to serve that mush the Quakers used to eat. I pushed it aside and demanded the sweet cereal I am so fond of. We started our little tug of war. She said, "No," and I started my whining and protesting. I don't always win everything, but I knew that I could at least get extra sugar in the mush. Besides, like the fellow said in the other article, it was not so important what I ate as it was that I start the day off establishing my autonomy. If you win the first battle of the morning, you have won the day.

But to my utter amazement, it didn't go at all like it was supposed to—like it usually did. When it was time for Mother to get red in the face and start jerking everything around, including me, she just smiled and said, "You can eat what is on the table or you can do without." I knew this was just round one, and that if I looked pitiful enough she would come around, but before I knew what was happening, she had lifted me out of the highchair and was cleaning the table. I stood there and let out a blood-curdling scream, and then I felt this awful sting on my bare legs. I didn't think she was mad enough yet to spank me. She usually waits until she totally loses patience and then strikes out in anger, but this time it almost looked as if she was smiling. She commanded, "Stop crying and go change your clothes." I let out another scream and "bam," another lick with that switch of hers. This was war! I couldn't let her get away with this; didn't she know I had control attachment disorder? I turned red in the face and screamed like I have never screamed before. This usually brought compromise, but instead, without another word of warning or threatening, "bam, bam, bam." I was shocked. My timid mother, whom I had such control over, was suddenly heartless. But after several more futile attempts that all ended at the end of a switch, I jumped up and ran to change my clothes. I never realized that she was so big!

When I came back and demanded something to eat, she told me

that in two hours I would be allowed to eat the Quaker mush, without sugar. I would like to say that I had learned my lesson and that in two hours I ate the stuff, but I didn't. I had trouble at lunch and again at supper. It was three days before I learned that Mother had taken my place as head of the house. I had to eat what she placed in front of me or starve. This was a different Mom from the one that I had been raising for two years. I couldn't make her mad, and it seemed that she had made up her mind to never let me win a single contest, for no matter what the issue, she quietly stuck by her word. She never let me overrule her. She was awesome!

It became a thing of certainty that if I whined, I would be denied all pleasure. You will find this hard to believe, but I learned that the only way to manipulate Mom was with a sweet smile and a carefully worded request. Anything else turned her into a broken vending machine—you couldn't get a thing out of her.

I had been used to her working herself up. All that disappeared. When she gave a command, she just gave it once. My hearing improved. I got to where I could hear a whispered command the first time. My survival depended on it. It was no longer a democracy. She stopped sharing power with me. I was made totally subject to her will.

Now, I noticed something right away. Mother seemed to like to read to me more. In fact, she started looking at me and smiling. I found it was wonderful. I really liked it. She looked at me like she really liked me. It had been a year since I had seen that beautiful smile that I loved so much. It made me feel better about myself. Whereas we had once been enemies, we could now be friends. Mother seemed to enjoy me when I was obedient. Of course, it was not my doing. She didn't leave me any choice but to obey. But it still felt good to be in fellowship with my mom. She would take me in her lap and we would just love each other like we used to do when I was just two months old. It was wonderful.

Oh, I found that in my weakness I still tried to dominate. It must be that theology thing again. I don't understand that yet, but I will let you know when I get it figured out. Until I do, it seems as if Mother and Father are not going to give me a chance to indulge my flesh— whatever that is. They talk about self-control. Between the switch and Mother's smile I have gotten pretty good at that self-control. By the way, have you tried Allfruit? It's pretty good in oatmeal. ☺

The Goo-goo Lady

I may be just fifteen months old, but I am not as dumb as my muttering makes me look. After all, I'm learning the King's English from adults who all talk like babies. When they talk to each other, it is easier to understand, but when they talk to us kids, they slobber and goo until we have to laugh at them. Then they are satisfied and go back to speaking to each other where you can understand them. But that's not what I wanted to tell you.

Just the other day, two ladies came to visit. They looked kind of funny, so I made the mistake of smiling at them. They couldn't keep their hands off me, so I started showing them all the things I could do. You should have seen me; it would have made Barnum and Bailey look like a church play. I guess that with all the attention I got a little rowdy, as Dad would call it, so he told me to go into the other room. I didn't want to leave my audience, so I tried an old trick that I had almost forgotten. It had never worked with Dad, but I had used it successfully against Mother on several occasions—that is until she read that second book—*No Greater Joy*, or something like that.

Anyway, when Dad commanded me to go outside and join my brothers and sisters, I saw the goo-goo lady look absolutely stricken. So I put on a forlorn, pleading look, placed one finger in my mouth, hung my head and shoulders, and started gently rocking from side to side on the balls of my feet. I saw it on "Shirley Temple." It worked well for her. I cut my eyes back to see how Dad was taking it, and he made a gesture toward his belt buckle. The ladies probably thought he was just scratching his belly button, but I knew better. I could not be sure that the presence of these two ladies would stop him from spanking me, so I decided not to take the risk. But as I headed out of the room, I got in one last shot. I cried just a little, so everyone would see how mean he was. The ouu-ahh lady jumped up and got right in front of me. She started making those unintelligible sounds that meant her reason had departed. I played it for all it was worth. My whimpers turned to sobs. She scooped me up and started saying things like, "pooooorrrrr baaaaabeeee, it'sss allll right. Therrre now. Sweet child." Then, looking from Dad to me, she put on her most sanctified, compassionate look and said, "She wants to stay, don't you dear?" I wiped my tears and tried to smile to show my appreciation. As she hugged me, I looked over her shoulder and saw Dad give Mom one of those "What do we do now looks?"

Mom jumped up and said, "Why don't we all go in the kitchen for a cup of hot tea?" I smiled and pulled on the lady's glasses, knowing I had won. Mom led the way, and the ladies followed. I had it all under control until I saw Dad step in front of my accomplice, and with a big smile he said, "I will take pumpkin; she may need to potty." He was smiling so sweetly with his mouth, but his eyes were chilled. Too late! He took me from the lady with the funny smell and then quietly shut the door to the kitchen. He sat me right back in the spot where I was sitting when he first commanded me to go outside. He went back to the chair where he had been sitting and quietly repeated his former command, "Go outside and play with the others." He didn't fool me. I could tell that he was not going to cut me any slack. I think he was hoping I would balk. I may be selfish, but I'm not stupid. I turned to flee toward the back door. He said, "Stop." I stopped and slowly turned. He said, "Smile." I smiled. He said, "Now go outside." I went.

A word from the editor: The story you just read is true, for I watched it unfold in my living room this past week. ☺

Dear Bro. and Sister Pearl,

I want to say how thankful I am for your example of child training. It seems almost revolutionary, yet it's also so obvious and logical. How could Christians have been missing it for so long?   T&D

Ramblin'

A young father dropped by to confer with one of my sons on some item of business. His little boy, not yet two years old, wandered over to the toy box and began to drag out all manner of interesting animals and colorful, noise-making contraptions. The men held our attention as they discussed several interesting items—everyone ignoring the kid. With business concluded, the father said to his son, "Come on, let's go." I am always observing the interaction of parents and their children, so I watched to see how quickly the little fellow would give up this capti-vating pile. It was obvious he had heard. But rather than drop the toys and come running, which is what you would expect from an obedient, well-trained child, he started grabbing toys as if he intended to prevent anyone from separating him from them. This young father and his wife have done a good job with their first child, and I was hoping for a good showing with this one as well.

I got much more than I hoped for. The wobbly toddler, with his arms full of toys, crossed the room to unburden himself at the toy box. He hastily made several trips until he had completely restored the room to its original order, and he then came to his daddy's side. I couldn't believe it. I quickly ushered them out of the house before my wife took notice. What if she considered the fact that this tiny tot was better trained than her husband? I know it is never to late to train, but it does get too late to want to be trained.

The most successful teaching is done before one year old. If you stake the plant when it is young, you won't end up trying to tie up a crooked plant—something I do most every year. As I have said before, "If a child is capable of taking toys out of a box, he is capable of put-ting them back in." Children are able to do much more, much earlier, than parents suppose.

Most training is actually untraining. That is, parents wait until a child is conditioned to inappropriate behavior before they commence training, and then they are trying to break bad habits, not develop good ones.

In our selfish, carnal state, we parents tend to be motivated by internal pressure more than wisdom—the pressure of feelings, frustra-tions, guilt, anger at being ignored, embarrassment, etc. We follow the path of least resistance. We tolerate more than we should until emotional pressure motivates us to action. The problem is that at that point our response is a negative one. It is criticism and irritation. The child understands that it is a competition between his parents and himself. I know the child can't put a name to it, but his little soul will respond to emotional control and manipulation just as would your spouse. An irritated parent comes across as a bully, like an incompatible roommate, rather than a dignified authority that is training for the child's good.

All early training is done by soliciting the child's participation in a repetitive manner, not by precept. You cannot lecture a one- or two-year-old on his duty. Threats and spankings will not mold habits. But if, right from the start, you never allow a child to leave his toys or clothes scattered, you will never have a hassle. Do not force the one-year-old child to work for you. Don't put pressure on children that young. You need to apply pressure if he is angry and throwing a fit, or stubbornly rebelling, but you don't pressure a child for being untrained. It's your fault.

So you shouldn't spank him for failure to put his toys up. Sit with him on the floor and make a game out of cleaning up. The first few times, it is not necessary that he do any significant portion of the work. You just want to communicate the idea that toys are never left scattered. Show him how to return toys to the box, laugh, sing, and play. You may

put away ten toys while he cleans up only one. You may have to hold his hand and guide it. He will think it is the grandest thing in the world to be playing with mother. If you make cleanup delightful, he will dump the toys out and then pick them up several times during the course of play.

Heed this warning: If you try to train in a confrontational attitude, the child will emotionally draw back from you and from the experience of cleanup. He will come to associate cleanup with tension and anxiety. You will not only fail to teach him to cleanup after himself, you will teach him to avoid clean up, and you will teach him to be tense and demanding of you. You would expect that a child living under a significant amount of parental tension and pressure would draw away from the parent, but the response is one of whining, demanding, clinging, and a generally dissatisfied state of mind. He will demandingly snuggle up with a frown on his face. He will forcibly push away things that you offer him, because his soul is dissatisfied and angry. He wants and needs unconditional affection given in the security of authority. What he has gotten is arbitrary rule with conditional affection given in an atmosphere of criticism and rejection—a sure formula for shipwreck.

As I was writing this I was interrupted by a child screaming. Deb was baby-sitting an eleven-month-old little boy. I let him scream for about five minutes, as I wrote the last lines of the above paragraph, and then I left my office and went to investigate. Deb was doing business on the phone—talking to a missionary, long distance. The child was clawing at the back door, trying to get it open so he could go outside. I picked up a switch and walked over to where he was conducting his scream-in. In a calm but firm voice I said, "No, stop crying." I didn't expect him to respond, but I wanted to establish the rules. When he failed to respond, I switched him twice on the only exposed skin—about three inches between his sock and pants leg. Again he did what I expected, what he does when his mother swats him—screams in defiance. But I have seen her swat him, and it never even gets his attention, other than a signal to scream louder. But when I switched his bare skin, he looked shocked and started to rub it. He continued to cry in protest, so I gave him two more licks on his bare leg. This time, he was convinced that I meant business. I know that he understood the issue, because he crawled past me, away from the door. Again I commanded him to stop crying, brandishing the switch. He stopped crying immediately, continuing to rub his leg while staring at me.

At this point, you could say that I had won. I had trained him to respond to my command and to cease his crying protest. But that is only the negative side of training. I like to stop with the positive, so I picked up one of the toys and started talking about it and trying to get his attention to something creative. The rule is **"When you take something away from a child, always replace it with something positive."** I don't mean that you should purchase compliance with a bartered settlement. You do not want to give the child an indulgence to satisfy him. Just don't leave him sitting in a boring vacuum. Turn him to something stimulating and creative. I didn't want to leave him sitting on the floor, rubbing his sore leg and brooding over his defeat. If I did that, he would soon return to his demand, for he had his heart set on going outside. After failing to gain his interest in the toys, I rolled a ball over to him. He shoved it away violently. It was a symbolic rejection of me and my attempt to distract him. At this point I might have spanked him for his little show of defiance and self-will, but I did not want to get caught in a downward attitude spiral. He needed to be drawn into something positive, so I overlooked that little display in hopes of turning his attitude around. I could have over ridden his temper and crushed his rebellion, but I wanted a friend, not just an obedient servant.

Sitting nearby was a five-gallon plastic water container, one third full of coins—our life savings—our insurance policy—our hospitalization—our retirement—former math curriculum—and now kiddy entertainment. Earlier he had reached down inside, as only his little hand could do, and drawn out some coins which were now scattered on the floor. I pretended to ignore him and commenced to pick up coins, making as much jingling sound as possible, and dropping them one by one back into the container. It was more than he could stand. He rushed over to where I was and reached deep into the jar, coming out with a hand full of coins. He handed them to me smiling. I took them and again dropped them back into the jar one by one. He drew out more and dropped a few on the floor, threw some across the room laughing, and handed me some. His attitude had recovered. He was happy. He was playing. He was no longer trying to get out the back door. I had not only won the contest of wills, I was winning his soul to myself. I was tying the strings of fellowship. This camaraderie would make it harder for him to disobey. He was coming to value my friendship. He would now want to please me.

But there was more. Now that I had him on more pleasant terms, I would teach him responsibility. I would teach him to clean up after himself, to put the coins back into the container. So I picked up the coins from the floor and held them over the hole, dropping them slowly so he could see what I was doing. I made it look and sound fun. After a moment, he touched the coin in my hand just as it slipped away into the jar. I then bragged on how smart he was to put the coins back in the container. Again I manipulated him into assisting me in returning the coins. He got the idea and retrieved a coin from the floor to return it to the jar. As he dropped the coin in the jar, he looked up for my approval, giving me a big smile. I bragged on his maturity and hard work, and dropped more coins in the jar. He was convinced; putting them back in the jar was as fun as taking them out. All this occurred to the background sound of my commands accompanying his actions. When he dropped a coin in the jar, I would say, "Put the coins in the jar." He came to identify my pleasant command with the pleasure of putting the coins back in the jar. He will now repeat the cleanup experience just to relive the pleasure of camaraderie. And he also learned the meaning of the command, "Put the coins back in the jar."

This took about ten minutes of my time. You say, "I don't have that much time." Then give your children to someone who does. Obviously you have chosen to dedicate your time to some pursuit you deem more valuable than well-trained children. You shouldn't be a parent if you are not going to give it all that these little developing souls deserve. The world has enough misfits without Christians adding to the mob. There is no greater joy than training up godly, emotionally stable, hardworking, and ministering children.

You are too busy? Amish mothers make their own soap, carry water in buckets, build a fire outdoors under a big cast iron pot, boil the clothes for thirteen kids and a grimy husband, hoe the garden, preserve the vegetables, kill and clean the chicken, milk the cows and churn the butter, split the firewood, and then do all the housecleaning chores that you do, and they have time. But then, they don't have telephones or TVs, and when visitors come over they don't stop work to visit. The visitor helps with the work.

I forget to mention this: The Amish mother trains her children to work! She is not their servant. She is the TRAINING BOSS. You can be too. It will take a load off your mind and body while building character and self-confidence in your children. ☺

My Journey

by Michael Pearl

In my journeys I came to an old wooden bridge. A traveler was halted by a bridging plank that was out of place. He asked my advice, so I stopped and helped him repair the single board. He traveled on, but before I could go far, others sought my assistance. Somehow over a period of time, after several successful repairs, I must have assumed responsibility for that bridge. I stood by it to assist and advise concerned travelers. After replacing the same surface boards several times, I came to realize that the problem was deeper. The supporting timbers were poorly constructed and now in a state of decay. At first I was thrilled to have discovered the cause. But it didn't take long to learn that the problem went all the way to the foundation. Once I got to the very bottom, I could stand in one spot and trace the failing structure right to its foundations. I was now quite certain as to the root cause of the failing roadway above. Yes, my analysis was quite certain. Yet, when I informed travelers that their poor journey was due to the foundation that had been laid, they did not seem as satisfied as I was. "How do we fix it," they asked. "Well, next time lay a better foundation," was an answer that came easily. "Yes, but what of this bridge?" they asked. "How do you safely re-lay the foundation of a bridge already carrying travelers?" I haven't come up with any certain answers for that one. I am better at analysis. It is a more popular profession. But I answer, "Very carefully, one timber at a time." "Which one first?" they ask. "You are putting a lot of responsibility on me; it is not my bridge." "But you are the bridge keeper," they accuse. "No, I am just a voluntary consultant who doesn't know as much as he did when he started." ☺

Index

Accusation–48
Addiction–21
Affection–49
Anger–1,3,9,14,17,19,20,21,24,25,26,27,30,37,40,44,45,46,48,58,71, 72,76,77,78,84,86,90,91,94,98,100
Attitude–2,11,16,18,24,365,40,76,87,90,100,101
Authority–20,21,27,29,31,47,48,56,88,90,91,92,99,100
Adversary–40
Birth control–69
Bitterness–2,4,16,47,75
Blame–20,48
Blessing–16
Bondage–18,77
Boundaries–3,31,59
Brat–25
Bully–40,99
Breast-feeding–66
Chaos–1,29,55
Character–87,102
Chastisement–25
Cheerful–18
Circumstance–4
Compassion–26
Compliance–45,57,61,73,89,101
Compromise–26,48,94
Condemnation–16
Condition–71,81
Confidence–39
Conflict–16,46,47,48
Contention–16
Control–26,44,46,47,56,60,70,88,90,94,99
Consistent–18,35,44,45,48,57,61,90
Criticism–17,48,99
Conviction–48
Deceit–42
Defiance–39,40,52,44,100
Disagreement–47
Diet–17
Discipline–26,27,29,31,36,44,45,48,61,88
Disobedience–35
Dissension–47

Divorce–74,75,78,79,80
Domination–46,70,71,72,91,95
Duty–30,71,85,86,99
Encouragement–18
Example–35,36
Expectation–13,45,48,51,52
Fear–25,32,40
Fellowship–17,22,55,57,58,59,95,101
Forgiveness–16,76,77,80
Free expression–26
Frustration–24,25,71,72,98
Godliness–45
Grace–16,17,36,90
Guilt–16,19,21,56,88,98
Happiness–3,4,86
Holiness–35,61
Honor–30,36,44,76
Hostility–25,26,71
Hypocrisy–35,70
Independence–26
Indulgence–8,70,83,84,86,87,88,91,92,93,101
Injustice–20
Insensitive–59
Instruction–31
Intimidation–3,72,91
Irritable–36,99
Joy–1,2,3,4,5,17,18,50,77
Joy of the Lord–4
Justice–20,48
Kindness–17
Law–15,20,25,27,29,56,59,60,76,80
Lazy–43,47,83,84
Love–17,20,25,26,27,30,35,47,48,56,65,70,76,77,80,88,90,95
Manipulation–26,88,99,101
Mercy–16,35,36
Obedience–7,10,17,26,39,48,61,76,95,98
Patience–25
Peace–18,26,27,52,77
Permissiveness–26,59
Pressure–19,49,99
Pity–71
Pleasure–86,102

Pride–71
Priorities–52
Program–71
Rebellion–10,27,40,45,47,49,54,56,61,91,92,99,101
Rebuke–15,45,58
Reconciliation–40
Relationship–3,45,56,75
Religion–5,18
Rejection–24
Repent–75,80
Reproof–27
Respect–30,35,39,40,49,50,52,56,57,58,76,77,86
Responsibility–17,73,80,83,88,102,103
Righteousness–36,61
Rod–5,10,27,32,45,54,55,61
Role model–2
Secrets–42
Security–27,56
Self-control–39,46,47,60,80,86,89,95
Self-denial–26,82
Self-discipline–35,61
Self-image–73
Self-will–39,73
Selfishness–20,26,30,31,35,85
Spanking–9,10,21,22,23,35,40,44,45,52,54,56,72,94,97,99,100
Spoiled–30,85
Standards–11,13,14
Stress–25
Struggle–44,48,73,82,85,86,87
Surrender–39,73
Subjection–76
Switch–27,36,56,65
Temper–25
Tension–47,49,52,100
Trust–18,56,59
Turmoil–29,75
Unruly–1
Values–17,60
Vanity–17
Virtue–71
Vision–52

Would you like answers to these questions?

How do I take the frustration out of homeschooling?

How do I stop being angry with my children?

What can I do about sibling rivalry?

Is it too late for my teenagers?

How can I teach my children to share, to give up their rights?

How do I get my children to sit still in church?

And much more: Potty training, lying, fighting, pouting, whining, how to use the rod, problems at puberty, teenage boys, teaching children to work, fairness, bad attitudes, husband and wife relationships, and more.

Written over a period of three years, the questions the Pearls were most asked are answered in these two books. They contain 81 individual articles, each on a separate subject. They are full of real-life, humorous stories illustrating the Biblical approach to training children. These exciting books also make great gifts. Or, reach out to your community by placing them in Doctors' offices and waiting rooms with your name and phone number on the inside cover. Order eight at a 40% savings and share them with your friends. Order your books from:

No Greater Joy Ministries, Inc.
1000 Pearl Road
Pleasantville, TN 37147

FREE subscription to our bi-monthly magazine with order

Books by Michael & Debi Pearl

Order Form 2001

BOOKS		QTY.	EACH	TOTAL
To Train Up a Child	1-7 BOOK		4.00	
To Train Up a Child	8-99 BOOKS		2.50	
To Train Up a Child	BOX of 100		2.20	
No Greater Joy Volume One 1-7 BOOKS Volume discounts same as To Train Up a Child			4.00	
No Greater Joy Volume Two 1-7 BOOKS Volume discounts same as To Train Up a Child			4.00	
No Greater Joy Volume Three 1-7 BOOKS Volume discounts same as To Train Up a Child			4.00	
Rebekah's Diary 1-7 BOOKS Volume discounts same as To Train Up a Child			4.00	
By Divine Design 1-7 BOOKS Volume discounts same as To Train Up a Child			4.00	
Repentance Doctrinal studies by Michael Pearl			3.50	
Romans Verse by verse commentary by Michael Pearl			8.00	

Name_____

Address_____

City_____ State____ Zip_____

Sub total	
Postage	
Total	

SHIPPING

$0.01 - $10.00	...add $2.50 S/H
$10.01 - $25.00	...add $4.06 S/H
$25.01 - $50.00	...add $5.85 S/H
$50.01 - 100.00	...add $8.00 S/H
$100.00 or more	...... add 8% S/H

All foreign orders, including Canada, triple S/H

- *No phone-in orders*
- *No CODs*
- *No charge cards*
- *US funds only*

www.NoGreaterJoy.org

No Greater Joy Ministries, Inc.
1000 Pearl Road
Pleasantville, TN 37147